p. 54 networks

# ACADEMIC COMPUTERS IN SERVICE

*Effective Uses for Higher Education*

*Charles Mosmann*

# ACADEMIC

# COMPUTERS

# IN

# SERVICE

Jossey-Bass Publishers

San Francisco • Washington • London • 1973

ACADEMIC COMPUTERS IN SERVICE
*Effective Uses for Higher Education*
   by Charles Mosmann

Copyright © 1973 by Jossey-Bass, Inc., Publishers
                   615 Montgomery Street
                   San Francisco, California 94111

Published and copyrighted in Great Britain by
                   Jossey-Bass, Ltd., Publishers
                   3 Henrietta Street
                   London WC2E 8LU

Library of Congress Catalogue Card Number LC 72-13602

International Standard Book Number ISBN 0-87589-161-6

Manufactured in the United States of America

JACKET DESIGN BY WILLI BAUM

FIRST EDITION

*Code 7304*

The
Jossey-Bass Series
In Higher Education

# PREFACE

Imagine the crisis and concern if the concept of the library—a collection of documents and other information services for the entire academic community—were just emerging for the first time. Matters we now consider standard procedure would loom as questions for careful analysis: Who will have access to the library? How will conflicts be resolved when two people want the same book? At what level should policy be established? How will the library be paid for? Should a per-use charge be made or should it be funded out of overhead? Is NSF or USOE interested? Should there be several specialized libraries or a single central one? Where should the library be located? How should it be administered? Should the college invest in the generation of an indexed catalog of its collection? In what form and to what level of detail? Should the college share with other institutions the burden of operating the library? Or should the college go it alone? What is Harvard doing? After numerous faculty committees considered these questions, the final plan would likely be so complex and so costly that it would be suggested that the entire project be abandoned or postponed indefinitely; yet the pedagogical value of the library would be so great as to make it absolutely essential to establish one at once.

Computation is a resource as useful and as vital to the intellectual health and operation of the college as the library. Its management, however, is little understood, as suggested by the fanciful analogy above. In an age of intense specialization, the computer is a device of such unique generality that in using it the scientist rubs shoulders with the humanist scholar, the creative artist, the administrator, the bookkeeper, and the growing numbers of students seeking access to it. When services are used this widely, how should they be provided? What other institutions can serve as models? How will the various users, with their conflicting demands and divergent goals, be protected from each other in their struggle for service?

John Caffrey and I reviewed some of the problems of managing and using computers in higher education. In 1967 the American Council of Education published our analysis in *Computers on Campus*. We examined some of the alternatives available at that time, making a particular effort to present in simple and straightforward terms the issues the administrator had to deal with. I view *Academic Computers in Service* as a sequel to that earlier book, for the growth of the computer field, the introduction of fast and cheap machines and of new languages, has not antiquated the bulk of the recommendations in *Computers on Campus*.

But many colleges now face more difficult—and sometimes completely different—problems than those they faced then. Demands for computation continue to grow in an era of dwindling funds; a wide spectrum of computer services is now available; the problems researchers (and students too) now want to solve require sophisticated techniques and machines.

*Academic Computers in Service* deals with these second and third generation problems. It is a practical handbook for administrators and for students and faculty performing administrative functions. The first five chapters depict the environment of modern academic computing. First, a brief case is made for the critical importance of computation for higher education. Chapter Two attempts to portray the complexity of user requirements, for the computing service is not like bread: all users cannot be served with slices from the same loaf; needs differ and requirements often conflict. Chapters Three and Four portray the complexity of the services that may satisfy these needs. Chapter Five concludes this survey by indicating that good management may be able to build sturdy, even economical, bridges between alternative needs and alternative services.

The rest of the book depicts the attendant problems and issues in detail, covering matters of management and use in administrative and academic services. The chapter titles indicate the nature of the issues to be faced. They begin with matters of the management of computing resources, in terms of organization, policy, and finance. The use of computers in instruction and administration is then addressed. Chapter Eleven touches on some of the technical issues, and the final chapter presents a brief overview of the terrain that has been covered, together with some consideration of what the future holds.

The descriptions of documents, services, and other resources at the ends of most chapters guide the reader to additional information on the topics treated. At the end of the book is an extensive bibliography with full citations for all the documents referred to and also a list of all the organizations known to me that provide services that may be of use in relation to computers in higher education.

More people have helped me write this book than I have space to acknowledge. In the several years I have been interested in the subject, I have visited scores of colleges, pried into their affairs, listened to their gossip, and carried away copies of their memos, reports, and plans. I have attended lectures, seminars, meetings, and those curiously formal "informal discussion groups." In the process of writing this book I interviewed perhaps a hundred individuals on college campuses, in federal and state government, and in the offices of foundations and associations. Rather than list all the people who have helped to educate me, it seems better to protect their identity except in cases of direct citation or quotation. Although anonymous, they have my gratitude.

However, some debts must be acknowledged. My friend and colleague John Caffrey, now executive vice-president of Rockland

County Community College, has been generously open with his unfailing wit and untiring advice. Mary and Risi, Jane, and the Cricket have patiently endured my concentration on what must often have seemed an alien and selfish task. I owe a debt of gratitude to the Exxon Education Foundation and to its executive director, Frederick deW. Bolman, for a grant to support site visits and field research. The Interuniversity Communication Council (EDUCOM) kindly consented to administer this grant. Neither of these organizations, I hasten to add, had any influence on the content: there the burden is strictly mine.

*Balboa Island, California*          CHARLES MOSMANN
*January 1973*

# CONTENTS

11.  Acquiring Systems                           146

12.  Computers for Innovation and Service        162

     List of Organizations                       170

     Bibliography                                173

     Index                                       181

# ACADEMIC COMPUTERS
# IN SERVICE

*Effective Uses
for Higher Education*

# 1

# COMPUTERS AS A SERVICE TO EDUCATION

For nearly a quarter century now, computers have been a glamorous new adventure in education, so increasingly useful, so seemingly limitless in potential, that the answer to almost every question has been yes. But many changes are taking place, and a hard, conservative reevaluation is now emerging.

In a recent interview, one college president expressed this change by saying, "We have come to the Dirty Question Phase: Where are all the dollars going? What is the educational value of what we are getting back? What alternatives do we have to what we are doing now?" At many institutions, administrators have been asking (and have been asked) these hard questions. Meaningful

1

answers have not always been those which faculty and students sometimes feared. Evaluations have not called for less computing or even necessarily for less money for computing. But they have requested cheaper computing and even better computing—computing services that match the real needs of the whole community rather than what some users feel campus users ought to need.

The nature of this question-asking and evaluating of alternatives absorbs most of the following chapters. But first I will survey the reasons for the continuing and growing convictions that computing is a vital part of higher education and that computers offer unique services to colleges and universities, services central to their proper role and function. Thus, before describing the new problems, I review the old ones.

The digital computer first emerged as a machine with limited functions in the applied mathematics involved in computing numerical tables. The first experts, those who built and used the machines, estimated that half a dozen of these computers might meet all requirements for computation. But they were wrong. The amount of computation that half a dozen of these early machines could do is now often exceeded by that needed by students alone at relatively small colleges.

Experts have gradually realized that the computer can do more than it was designed for; its generality of purpose makes its potential difficult to understand and easy to underestimate. In a very real sense, it is the ultimate machine. While it cannot move a ton of earth or a railroad car or even a shuttle or a hoe, it can move symbols. And this manipulation of symbolic representations of information does something close to the jobs most people in an advanced society spend much of their time at. Any task that can be defined in these broad terms is a potential application of computers.

The first job of the computer in the academic community was as a research tool; it is now so entrenched in this role that many research activities will never be attempted without it again. The computer has participated, for example, in a fundamental change in scientific investigation. Contemporary with the development of the computer, many sciences changed from a primary concern with the complete understanding of simple phenomena (such as a single atom or cell) to an interest in understanding how these simple phenomena combine into complex systems: the states of energy in a crystal, the configuration of atoms in a protein molecule, the nervous responses involved in hearing. Insight into these phenomena require experiments that may result in thousands—even millions—of separate pieces of information. To sift through these data, sort them in various ways, perform statistical analyses of them would be an unimaginable burden without a computer.

Many people not closely associated with science have read James D. Watson's *The Double Helix* and have formed from it an impression of how people do science. They may be surprised to learn how the computer has changed the activities that were central to Watson's account. The book relates the parallel efforts to understand the structure of the DNA molecule by analysis of X-ray diffraction data and by building physical models that satisfy the structural requirements. Computers are now commonly used in both these activities. They can be used to control the X-ray experiments and analyze the resultant data, moving the crystal to a new position for a fresh experiment on the basis of data from the early ones. Computers do not build physical models out of cardboard sheets and metal rods, but they can sketch pictures of such models—perspective drawings, even stereopticon pairs to simplify viewing—from any angle the scientist selects.

The impact in the social sciences came later than that in the natural sciences and has not yet reached its full growth. The computer allows social scientists to manipulate with great facility large masses of information: to perform tasks in an afternoon that previously would have taken several years and been major research accomplishments. The simulation of social systems on a computer gives the social scientist what he has always lacked before—a laboratory analogous to that of the physical scientist, where events can be caused to occur and their results recorded, studied, and analyzed.

In the humanities, the effect has so far been tangential rather than direct. Lacking the financial resources of many of their scientific colleagues, humanists have naturally been cautious about the use of this machine. They have used it for work that can be automated easily but which is not necessarily the most important part of humanistic research: clerical work and the application of scientific methods to the raw materials of humanists. It will probably never again be economical to use hand labor in producing a concordance; the computer is not only faster and more accurate but also cheaper. The analysis of style is an aid in determining the authorship of questionable works and dating texts within an author's career. It is aided by a statistical analysis of minutiae of the documents: a composer's use of peculiar harmonic devices or cadences or the irregularities in a poet's use of rhyme or rhythm. Here too the computer is an invaluable assistant. The fact that computers have not found new interpretations of the novels of Melville and have not created major works of art does not denigrate the help they are providing in humanist studies.

In matters of education, the computer forms a new subject and also a new chapter in some very old subjects. The computer is a new kind of event in the universe; it raises basic and theoretical questions about the nature of purposeful processes and the structure of information. These questions have no natural place in any of the traditional disciplines, and a new one has had to be created, usually represented by a new department called Computer Science or Information Science. This department is likely to be an anomaly. It is neither a physical science nor a social science; it is emphatically not engineering as usually construed (although computer engineering may also be a subject of instruction and is a natural extension of electrical engineering). Simon (1969) suggests that it is one of several "artificial sciences" (paralleling the natural sciences).

Some institutions, particularly two year colleges, offer programs of vocational training associated with the computer; these are usually called data processing courses as distinguished from the theoretical computer science courses. Because the computer industry already has annual sales of twelve billion dollars in the United States alone, and grows at a rate of 16 percent, a steady supply of people with computer training will be required to serve it.

Although the computer science department has its own research interests and its own curriculum, one of its functions is to offer service courses to teach the rudiments of computer use to many students whose interest is not in the computer as such but in the use of computers in other areas, usually the physical or social sciences. In many fields in science, engineering, and business administration, the computer has become an essential part of the practitioner's bag of tools. An engineer or physicist or economist cannot be sent to find a job (or a position in graduate school) without some knowledge of how computers can be used effectively to solve the problems he will face. Hence engineering and physics and economics students are expected to pick up a smattering of computer know-how and to use it as appropriate in homework and class problems.

The computer's impact in some fields is much more drastic than this simple explanation may suggest. It is so much more powerful a tool than the adding machine, the slide rule, and mathematical tables that totally new pedagogical approaches can be taken. When students are to do exercises and problems by hand, the required calculations must not exceed the limited time available: a few hours per week, ten or twelve weeks per term. In physics, among other sciences, few real problems and few of the problems that students should learn to solve satisfy this requirement. Thus students are given a watered-down version of the science. The computer, by greatly enhancing the students' problem-solving abilities, allows the exercises they work to be close to real science; even undergraduates can work in the atmosphere of the research laboratory and receive training closely directed to the objective of making the curriculum relevant to future work.

Finally, the tools of the traditional disciplines can be applied to the computer. The computer is perhaps the most socially disruptive technology of all in its effect on employment patterns, on science and scholarship, on business administration and manufacture, and on our social institutions. Its history, its social impact, its philosophical status make it important to study. But before philosophers and sociologists and historians can make such studies, they must learn something about the computer, usually by trying to apply it to a quantitative problem and experiencing firsthand how the computer can affect the intellectual habits of its user.

Thus the computer arrives on campus through the front gates of research and instruction. But it also enters quietly via the back door of administration. A college is a business as well as many other things, and the use of computers in the administration of business enterprises is now firmly established. Unless the college is small indeed, it usually finds it worthwhile to investigate computer-based services for preparing the payroll and managing financial records. Often this activity involves little more than agreeing to allow the local bank or some other agency to use its programs and its computers to process the college accounts. Large schools are interested in using the computer to manage student records, to assist in the registration process, and to produce the class lists, student schedules, and statistical reports that would otherwise take many hours of typing. Beyond the conversion of such transactional or clerical tasks to computer processing, the administration may be interested in the further possibilities of having records accessible to the computer: making information about the college's past history and present condition available in a form in which it can be used effectively in planning and decision-making. The computer may not produce improved institutional research, but it makes it feasible within existing economic, temporal, and personnel constraints, thus fostering improved planning and resource allocation.

Some of the applications touched on in this survey are examined in detail in later chapters. Here I intend them only as background and justification for the assertion that the computer has indeed now been granted tenure; it has become a permanent part of the educational scene and central to the service of academic purposes.

It is instructive, in this context, to consider the financial situation briefly. In the first decade of computer use, the budget for it grew at such an astonishing rate that credible predictions seemed impossible to make. Later, in the 1960s, average annual growth rates of 40 to 50 percent in the computer budget were normal. But some of this increase was part of the growth of the institutions themselves; this was an era of rapid expansion of the university educational program and research establishment. The end of the sixties brought tight educational budgets that made necessary a realistic evaluation of many of the programs on campus and a decrease in budgets that had seen nothing but growth for a decade. The change in the pattern of computer expenditures is revealing. Annual increases in budgets for computing were down, by 1970, to 8 or 10 percent, but they were at least still increasing at many institutions, even though other budgets were shrinking.

The source of funds for computing further emphasizes the growing importance many institutions place upon this service. The total expenditure for computers in higher education in 1969–1970 was more than double that in 1966–1967—about $472 million. But during these years, the contributions of the federal government and private agencies (principally in the form of manufacturer discounts) decreased markedly; the slack was taken up by the institutions themselves.

In higher education, overall statistics such as these are usually so distorted by the large institutions that the small colleges may not be reflected at all. These colleges, where federal support for computers was never large, had been paying for their own computation. Here, too, expenditures tended gradually to increase or level off with more money or the same amount of money being spent for more computing service. However, because of good planning and management and intelligent decision-making, computer costs no longer threaten to overtake the college budget, even though more computing is being bought, to be used by more students in more courses offered by more departments. Perhaps at the small college even more than at the university the computer provides a unique opportunity to improve the quality of education and at a small marginal cost. At colleges large and small the faculty and administration realize that the computer is not just another scientific instrument and financial burden but rather that the intelligent use of computers in instruction can do more for the educational quality of a college than can a comparable investment almost anywhere else.

Another aspect of computing must be mentioned, although it is more difficult to speak of than educational quality, and that is campus politics. Computing is expensive and it is a critical resource for many functions that cut across all avenues of campus life. It thus represents influence and power, and a share in its control is jealously guarded by many. The assistant provost of a major private university said in a recent conversation, "The computer is really the center of all the damned political to-do on the campus. That's where the money is and that's where all the issues meet face to face. So many of the questions of where we are going and who's going to control what are fought out in the computer area. . . . Issues seem to get turned around and backed into the computer committee. It's a storm center. It's a good place to fight."

The computer thus is a peculiar challenge to the college

president and those about him whose responsibilities are allocating scarce resources among competing demands and making decisions about future programs on the basis of their understanding about the broad goals of the institution. The computer is a complex resource. Allowed to grow unchecked, it naturally absorbs as large a share of the budget as its promoters can lay hands upon; groping for analogy, several writers have independently come upon that of cancerous growth. But suppressed, it drives some of the brightest students and most valuable faculty away and depresses the quality of education.

Educators sometimes look for a formula in such cases: How many dollars per student? What percentage of the budget? But there is no simple way to ascertain the correct level; at least none has yet emerged. There is not even a simple way to set up a mechanism for evaluating computing, for it is like nothing else on the campus. Sometimes the chameleon machine looks like a scientific instrument or a laboratory tool (but not very often). Then one can make decisions about it just as though it were a microscope or specialized electronic gear. But sometimes it behaves like a library, a storehouse of services for any member of the campus community. At other times, it is a bookstore—a storehouse of resources for those who have the money and are willing to spend it for computing. Perhaps it is most analogous to a steam plant, manufacturing a product and sending it around the campus; but then many argue that it is a utility at heart and should be acquired and managed like an expensive form of electricity or telephone service.

The administrator attempting to deal with computer service may find its special and shifting characteristics bewildering. What appears to be a piece of machinery and a capital investment turns out rather to be a service and an on-going expense for which the various visible items of hardware are merely the tools. What begins as a product—a computer—ends up as a service—what I have been calling here computing and what is sometimes referred to as information services.

The administrator may throw up his hands and be tempted to leave matters to the technical experts. But the technical experts likely should not have control over this expensive and valuable resource. Although computing may need encouragement at some stages, it needs control at others. At all times, it needs to be channeled into fruitful usage and away from those marginal applications which ultimately make it a financial burden to the college. Faced with these dilemmas, the college president must resign himself to the fact that computing needs attention—his attention—if it is to be encouraged in the service of institutional goals.

Once computing demands and gets this attention, some basic questions emerge and must be answered. At some institutions, the basic questions take a rather simplified form and resolve to this primary one: How big a computer should we get? This question is wrong on several counts; rather than an answer, it deserves a reply in the form of several other questions.

*What kind of computing services do you want?* Computing services can be acquired in many ways. By no means do all of them involve having machinery visible on the campus or getting a computer.

*Why just one computer?* Another simplifying but possibly erroneous assumption is that all needs are basically the same and can be satisfied from the same source, like telephone service or electrical power. Unless the needs are modest and similar, perhaps having several sources of computing is a better solution than having just one. The most convenient computing service for students when they are just beginning to learn how to write programs in a simple language may not be convenient or economical for the registrar or for research projects in physics and sociology.

*What do you mean by big?* Big is often a circumlocution for expensive, and the question frequently means What can we afford? or even How much do we have to spend? To get beyond cost to a rational evaluation of alternatives, computing must be seen as having many dimensions (although all of them, it is true, must ultimately be judged in relation to cost). A machine is big enough if it fills needs; it is small if it does not. A "big" machine for some users may mean fast arithmetic; for others, lots of storage capacity; for others still, special languages and sophisticated processors.

Once the variables defining "how big" are quantified, additional issues appear, having to do with hardware, software, and management. If the amount of computation to be done is moderate, several possible configurations of hardware will satisfy the need: a single medium-sized computer that will meet all the needs, with some excess capacity for anticipated near-term growth; several small machines (sometimes called mini-computers) that can be dispersed geographically at the convenience of the users; or part of a large computer also available to users not associated with the college. Because it is possible to communicate with computers by means of telephone lines, this last alternative does not necessarily imply any geographic inconvenience to the users.

Software is the computer programs; they extend the usefulness of the computer (the hardware) by making it easy for the user to specify the functions he wishes to perform. Many new languages and program systems extend the use of computers in new directions, although they tend to be specialized; not all are available on all computers. Thus, opinion is bound to differ as to which machines are satisfactory and which are not. Computer X may meet the requirements of most of the anticipated campus users; but if it does not have the interactive language needed for student use or the statistical programs wanted by the social sciences, it is not a wise choice.

Beyond hardware and software, management concerns need to be discussed and evaluated. If the computer is to be on campus, it can be purchased outright or it can be leased from the manufacturer or a third party may be willing to buy it and lease it to the college. Other arrangements have been pursued at some institutions: a third party may be interested in locating its computer on the campus, leasing the college that portion of the available computer time the college can use and marketing the remainder to other agencies. If computation is to be provided by a large, off-campus facility, further alternatives exist. Service for administrative purposes can often be provided by banks and commercial service bureaus. For academic purposes, computing is available from commercial agencies anywhere in the United States (although in some rural areas communications costs may be high); regional educational centers offer their services in a number of localities; special cooperative ventures can also be initiated if none of the existing and available services is totally satisfactory.

Thus the range of alternatives is so great that almost any need can be satisfied in one way or another. The problem is, however, that institutions do not always know exactly what their needs are. Thus, they must first draw up a clear and specific list of requirements. The elements of such a list are the subject of the following chapter.

Since this chapter is broad in scope, perhaps it is useful to begin by listing publications of general interest that should be in any basic library on computers in higher education. Hammer (1957) although it is now rather out of date, was the first attempt to consider the special role of computers in higher education. The so-called Rosser Report, (*Digital Computer Needs in Higher Education,* 1966), tried to evoke some national norms and goals for educational computing. Some of its material is still pertinent and is often quoted. It was soon followed, however, by the "Pierce Report," (President's Science Advisory Committee, 1967), which made more detailed and specific recommendations; it was and remains a landmark and contains many valuable ideas. Roger Levien of the Rand Corporation made a third study of the national scene. His report (1972) contains a wealth of useful material, including a good introduction to the whole field of computers in education and an analysis of statistical data, as well as recommendations for action at the national level.

For a general introduction, Caffrey and Mosmann (1966) remains a good nontechnical survey of the needs of colleges and the problems they face in satisfying the need. It is written from the point of view of the individual institution rather than the national scene, which distinguishes it from the three reports just cited. Gerard (1967) is a conference report and contains some good papers, especially on the potential impact of computer-aided instruction. A special issue of the *Journal of Educational Data Processing* (1971) contains eight articles that together present a useful picture of contemporary issues.

John Hamblen of the Southern Regional Education Board has undertaken a series of statistical surveys of computers in higher education. The most recent of these (Hamblen, 1972) is of great value to any administrator who wants to see where his college stands against the national profile. The Levien book cited earlier contains a good analysis of the available data. Hamblen has also published a much briefer analysis of the data (1971). The American Association of Collegiate Registrars and Admissions Officers has also conducted periodic surveys of administrative use; their most recent report (AACRAO, 1970) is also a useful document to have.

This chapter also included a brief description of research computing. Since this topic is not covered elsewhere in this volume, a few general references here may be of interest to some readers. W. O. Baker (1970) is an excellent survey of the impact of the computer in science and is not too technical to be read by the general reader. *Scientific American* has published a series of articles that together form a good overall picture of computers and their impact: Oettinger (1966), Coons (1966), Greenberger (1966), and Suppes (1966). These are reprinted in *Information* (1966) and in *Computers and Computation* (1971).

# 2

# NEEDS OF USERS

When a university or college is considering the acquisition of computing service, responsible administrators try to determine the needs of the largest number of potential users on the campus. But when they ask these users for their requirements, a bewildering assortment of apparently incompatible needs emerges.

Professor A, who represents an influential group in chemistry and physics, has research problems that require large volumes of rapid mathematical computation. His programs will be written in machine language or FORTRAN. He regards all this business about time-sharing and remote access and new sophisticated languages as frills, not worth serious consideration.

Professor B intends to use the computer for instruction. He must have terminals accessible to his students, a good interactive language, and reliable performance, available twenty-four hours a day.

Professor C has been collecting data for three decades on variations in punctuation and spelling in the metaphysical poets. He

13

understands that computers can help him in the otherwise hopeless task of analyzing this vast accumulation of data. He would like service which would allow him to explain what he wants to an intelligent analyst, submit his data, and receive answers to his questions, within six months, if possible.

Professor D is a social scientist and will be pleased with any computer that has a good collection of statistical programs that he can use in his research and that his students can use in his courses. Because student use is intensive over short periods of time, D considers it critical that small student jobs be returned within one hour of their being submitted.

The comptroller insists that he will use a computer service in common with academic users only if he is guaranteed that (1) his work will have top priority (since the payroll is obviously the most important data processing job on the campus); (2) provision will be made for getting his work done on some other machine if the one on campus should be out of order when he needs it; and (3) the location and staff of the computer will be selected to guarantee the security of his data, programs, and reports.

Professor E teaches computer science courses. He argues the importance to the college of having one of the three recently announced computers of innovative design. He argues further that the staff should be minimal, so that users can do their own programming. Students should be able to get their hands on the machine without a lot of regulations and operating personnel impeding the primary educational function of the computer.

By the time the administrative committee has interviewed Professors Q, R, and S, the members may suspect the hopelessness of their task. Everyone wants the particular configuration of hardware, software, and policy that will best satisfy his needs. How can a reasonable compromise be found?

Perhaps the committee needs to be reminded that if one does not like the answers he is getting, he should consider changing the question. If each potential user describes the decision he wants from the committee, rather than the problem he wants the computer to solve, coordinated planning is impossible. To the user, what is of interest is ultimately a service and not a thing. The users should be asked to describe what they want the computer service to do for them. So that administrators can compare and coordinate these requirements, users should make their descriptions in terms of a common set of dimensions. Since computer service is a complex product, it cannot be described by two or three dimensions, as, for example, can telephone or electrical service. The small college selecting its first computer may need few dimensions and few concrete specifications, but a large institution may need to specify a dozen or more characteristics in order to obtain satisfactory computing service.

Here are some characteristics that may be important in describing user needs:

*Response time.* Once the user submits work to the computer, when will the job be completed and returned to him? For some research jobs, days or even weeks will do, while for the person writing and testing a new program, once per day is probably the upper limit. An hour or two may be the maximum students can afford to wait, depending upon the demands of their teachers. Administrative jobs will probably range from a few hours to many days. Turn around time, the time it takes to get a job back once it is submitted, is especially important if the user's next step depends on the output of a computer run. If, for example, the next experiment cannot be set up until the results of the prior one are known or if the next debugging run of a program depends on the results of a prior test, the user becomes impatient of delays, the degree of his impatience bearing a direct relation to the ratio between work time and wait time. If the experiment runs for ten days, a day's wait for the results of the computer run is not too long; if the programmer takes one hour to correct his program and submit another debugging run, a day's wait for results is very long indeed.

*Predictability.* How much of the computer work can be scheduled in advance? If a job is expected at a particular time and if its characteristics are known, it is easy for a computer center to respond quickly. Most administrative jobs, for example, are highly predictable: the jobs associated with student registration and preparation of class lists can be scheduled as soon as the dates for registration are set; the dates for monthly financial reports, payroll, and tax form preparation can be scheduled indefinitely into the future. Research and instructional use is harder to predict than are administrative jobs. When a research project begins, the investigator may be able to estimate the amount of computing he will want to do, but he may not be able to say in which months he will want to do it. While the length of potential student jobs cannot be predicted at all, the teacher should be able to predict how many students will need to use the computer for how many jobs and in which weeks their jobs are likely to be submitted.

*Turnaround reliability.* How serious a problem will be created if the job cannot be run as scheduled? Most work does not suffer critically if it is postponed a day or two, provided such delays are not very frequent. Administrators claim that their work requires absolute reliability, waving the red flag of the payroll. But few jobs require such reliability, although it is always desirable.

*Security.* Which data and programs should be retained in such a way as to minimize their availability to unauthorized personnel? No one is likely to want to sneak a look at the results of an X-ray diffraction analysis or to tamper with the results of a geopolitical simulation. However, some administrative data are sensitive, particularly those connected with students and staff. Certain data (grades, for instance) are even of enough interest that individuals may go to some lengths to attempt to modify them, unless this tampering is made both difficult and dangerous. Security should also be applied to the protection of unique copies of important records from accidental loss or damage. Important records should be duplicated, and one copy should be kept separate from the other.

*Interaction.* Will some jobs require that the user interact with the system during the time the computer is being used? Sometimes a user does not submit a complete description of the work the computer is to do, wait for the result, and continue his own work; rather, he interacts with the computer and makes further decisions when partial results are known. In computer-aided instruction, for example, the computer presents information to or selects a task for the student on the basis of student response to a question. Sometimes computers and laboratory equipment are linked so that the computer output is instructions for modifying the controls and continuing the experiment. Other jobs do not require this service but may be much facilitated by it. This interaction capacity is available only on computers dedicated to a single task or else on those with a time-sharing system.

*Access location.* How close to the office or laboratory or classroom must the service be? Is it a hardship to drive or take the bus to a remote location on the edge of the campus to get the work done? These questions obviously relate to the frequency with which jobs are to be submitted. For some jobs, however (as in the experimental control example above), the service must be available at the precise spot where the data are available; next door is not good enough. If an interactive computer program is to be used as part of a classroom demonstration, the service must be where the class is.

*Quantity.* How long will the job take? How much of the computing resources will it absorb? These seem like simple questions, yet answering them is difficult, especially outside the context of a particular machine. The preparation of an administrative report may require twenty minutes per week on an IBM 360/40. If the computer is twice as fast and powerful as the 360/40, the job takes ten minutes, and so on. However, extrapolation from one machine to another is not always this easy. A small computer may make it necessary to perform the process less efficiently, thus requiring a great deal more time than one would expect by straightforward extrapolation. Similarly, a sophisticated computer might present alternatives to make the process more efficient still. Despite its difficulty, this is a characteristic of great importance since it defines the size and speed of the computer required to get the job done.

*Service level.* What levels of assistance will be expected by the various users? Different users (and the same user doing different things, or at a different experience level) ask for different levels of assistance from the computing center staff. One user may be satisfied if he is simply given a key to the room where the computer is housed, so that he can run his jobs by himself. Another may want nothing to do with the machinery: he wants a window where he can deliver his input and receive the computer output. Another wants programmers to whom he can describe his problems in his own terms. Almost all users, unless they are professional computer scientists, want assistance at various times in overcoming technical difficulties and in utilizing the complex capacities of the computer. Specialists in various computing techniques of interest to the user community thus form an important part of the computing service.

*Special hardware needs.* Will some of the anticipated use influence the machinery required? If users plan to produce maps, graphs, or pictures of any kind, special devices are necessary. A printer capable of producing lower-case letters and special characters may be justified. Special input devices can read mark-sense pages or even printed characters. Caution must be taken in evaluating the statement of a user that he needs the XYZ/123 machine, however. Usually at least a few other ways of solving his problem can be found.

*Special software needs.* Will some users need particular languages or types of language? A so-called general-purpose language is often hard for the average customer to use because of its complexities. The special languages perform a much smaller range of functions, but they do them simply and well. Also, not all languages are suitable for student use, while the production of computer-aided instructional materials is much enhanced by the use of one of the languages designed for that purpose. Users who plan to perform mathematical or statistical work insist on an adequate set of programs and routines. Some users make a case for exotic systems: information management systems, simulation packages, and specialized programs. Even when these are available for a given computer, they may have to be purchased or leased separately from the hardware.

Users are naturally concerned about the policy that will guide the management of the computer service. If the user has his own computer in his own laboratory or office, he can ensure that the computer will be used to meet his needs most effectively. But if the campus director of computing services is to control the resource, how can the individual user be sure that his needs will be met? Questions of allocation, long-range stability, and user influence in decision-making in particular should concern him.

When enough computer time is available for everyone who wants it, few serious problems arise among users. When the system becomes congested, however, some work must be postponed or canceled. Before a user commits himself and his work to a computer system, he should know how resources will be distributed when they become scarce. Many users have learned by bitter experience that computer directors and managers promise them anything in order to get them to fill the idle time on their machines. But when the hours and minutes and seconds are no longer idle, the promises may not be worth much. Then the professor's students complain that they cannot do their work, the administrative clerks complain that the information they need is not at hand, the researcher gets behind schedule on his NIH study, and the president asks where his monthly budget report is. Wise users know that the policy on allocation must be set before the problems are on the doorstep; such a policy is the user's only guarantee of the availability of service in the long run.

Long-range planning is another policy area of great importance. The sophisticated user may not be willing to place total dependence on a campus-wide computing agency because experience has taught him that as requirements change and improved systems become available, the hardware system will soon be traded in for a new one. If the new one is not compatible with the old, much of the user's investment in programming may be in jeopardy. He does not want to make this investment unless he has assurance that his problems and plans will have weight in the decision to change systems when this decision has to be made.

Since every possible problem cannot be foreseen and accounted for, the most important commitment the administration can make is to a procedure that assures user influence over the development of policy as new situations arise. Allocation of resources under congested conditions, long-range shifts in system design, funding and pricing considerations, and the like need to be reappraised continually, and the user wants to have a share in these discussions.

One user stands apart from the others: the computer scientist. His needs must be evaluated carefully and his relationship to other users must be considered critically, for he may be at odds with them in a number of ways. All other users consider computing a vehicle for investigating interests beyond the computer. But to the computer scientist, the computer itself is the subject of investigation, and the jobs he runs are his experiments. He wants to study alternatives to the systems that other users regard as stable and given. Since novelty and variety are of greater interest to him than sta-

bility and consistency in computer service, he may want to under-
take radical redesign and implement innovative methods. In fact,
one computer center director suggests that the computer scientist
views a computer system as a bucket of parts, to be shaken up and
assembled in different ways, and that this scientist naturally takes an
interest in all the computation on campus, since a big bucket of parts
is much more interesting than a small one.

If the computer scientist's particular interests are understood
and if policies are established to buffer him from the other users,
the situation can be controlled. However, some computer scientists
claim that they are best able to serve as directors of campus computing because they know more than anyone else about the technical
aspects of the system. Unfortunately, a computer science faculty
member serving as director of computing services has almost without exception been an unhealthy situation, impeding the growth
of intelligent use by members of other departments. Although the
computer scientist knows more about hardware and software, he
does not know more about the needs of other users or about the
management of the resource. In almost every case, the wisest
course is to refuse this offer of leadership; the computer science
department and the computer service must be kept at arm's length:
better ways exist to satisfy the needs of the computer scientist than
to give him the key to the store.

So far, I have discussed how user requirements can differ
from one another in a number of different dimensions, all of which
must be considered in order to reach a proper understanding of
the total campus computing requirement. The computing system
selected must, as far as possible, be broad and flexible enough to
cover the entire scope of the requirements submitted and judged
worth meeting. This is not a trivial task, but neither is it an
impossible one. Many users can be grouped very closely: none has
requirements that are not common to all. The plans of some users are
so flexible that they can fit into several radically different environ-
ments equally well. In fact, the requirements of most campus users
are highly predictable. The following paragraphs describe examples
of common computer uses which a great many users employ at one
time or another.

*Debugging.* Virtually all users write programs that must be tested, or debugged. Regardless of the purpose of these programs, the requirements of their test runs are much the same, in that they call for small amounts of computer time, demand fast turnaround, and are essentially unpredictable. Interactive computing is useful for this purpose but not absolutely necessary, unless the finished program is to be interactive. Requirements for reliability and security are low, even for administrative debugging.

*Student use.* Student programs follow a pattern like debugging, since much of their activity is writing and testing programs that are used only once.

*Scientific use.* Scientific research uses many different kinds of computing but tends to rely mostly upon large quantities of fast computation with relatively small input and output requirements. Such computing is called number crunching by the professionals, because it contains huge amounts of arithmetic and little else. However, it constitutes only a portion of scientific use. For computers used interactively in experimentation, for example, the requirement is usually for very fast response, on the order of tenths or hundredths of seconds, but not for extensive computation. Some scientific applications produce graphic output of considerable sophistication.

*Social science use.* Users in the social sciences are likely to use large and elaborate programs which may have been developed elsewhere (simulations and games, information management systems, and so on) and extensive data bases (such as federal census data, now available on magnetic tape). These programs usually require long but productive blocks of computer time.

*Computer-aided instruction.* Involving the computer directly in the student's learning process requires interactive service, special terminal hardware, and high reliability. The requirements are generally independent of the discipline being taught, although graphic (as opposed to purely alphanumeric) display capability is more critical in some subjects than others.

*Administration use.* Administrative users have fairly strict requirements for high reliability and security. Their work is relatively predictable (except for debugging). Interactive use is not critical, although if available it can often be used effectively. Because of the security requirements and the amount of input and output, location of access may be important.

None of these examples is intended to be all-inclusive or to characterize every user. The work of some physicists may have characteristics of social science use, while some administrative applications are more like science uses. Yet for a given institution these examples could be extended and refined. They might then be combined into clusters indicating common interests and common requirements. An analysis of requirements for computing services at Harvard University concluded, in fact, that six categories sufficiently accounted for their work (Austin, 1971): (1) User written program compilations and executions, corresponding to what we have called debugging above. (2) Package programs, such as simulation games or statistical analyses, which are used especially in the social sciences. Essential for these programs is a computer on which the existing programs can be run. Also, the appropriate languages, input/output facilities, and the like must be available. (3) Large scientific production, characterized by requirements for large capacity and high speed. (4) Administrative production, requiring dependable scheduling with a high level of security and reliability. Administrative use is characterized by large amounts of input and output relative to the computation performed. (5) On-line data collection and process control, referring primarily to laboratory use of computers as part of the experimental apparatus. The demand for reliability and responsiveness makes it difficult for most common services to satisfy the need. (6) On-line interaction, which implies some special hardware and software characteristics, including a variety of languages and other software systems. Interactive users (other than students) tend to want an ever-increasing volume of programs and data, which implies a considerable investment in storage media.

In many institutions one or more of these classes can be dropped, while other institutions have to divide one or more of the classes into additional categories. The Harvard analysis gives little consideration to service level, which is likely to be high at institutions smaller than Harvard. In general, however, an institution should be capable of describing its computing needs in terms of six or so categories. The list varies at the same institution over the years as needs change and as users grow in knowledge and sophistication.

In making such an analysis, we must bear the "menu prin- ciple"' in mind: what is available influences what people want. Some campus computer centers tell visitors that "no one on this campus has any need for interactive service," meaning, in fact, that there has never been any interactive service and so the users have learned how to do their jobs some other way. Since they do not know much about it or how they would use it, they do not demand it. Such use is, then, being suppressed. The impact of this suppres- sion on computing effectiveness cannot be easily evaluated.

Finally, the analysis must take into account not only present but future requirements. Planning only for the computation that would be used if the service were available later this week is point- less. The plan must attempt to satisfy interests and demands as these change over the next few years, a difficult task anywhere, but par- ticularly so in schools relatively new to computing. Many of the professors and administrators who today claim they have no need for any computation in the foreseeable future will change their minds quickly and radically when they see what some of their colleagues are accomplishing. Many who have in mind only a single application will be inspired by its success to think of twenty more. Some professors, encouraged by the success of their use of the computer, will be followed in the next academic year by all their students. In such cases, prediction is probably best made on the basis of the experiences of similar institutions in similar circum- stances, but a few years ahead. Their examples can indicate what the school new to computing will be doing a few years later. The direction of demand is fairly easy to predict, although not its rate. Once computing is established on the campus and is used in several ways by several departments, users begin to demand a greater quantity of computation, as more applications and more difficult tasks emerge; faster reaction time, as more of the users' work comes to depend on the completion of each computer job; more interac- tive service, with greater terminal variety; more convenient access; and greater variety of user services, including both software and available consultation.

In summary, the characteristics a user expects of the computer service available to him are complex but can usually be clustered into half a dozen centers of interest. The computer service for any campus must be tailored to institutional needs and to the interests of its campus users, which in turn depend on the character of the institution and on the experience level of its staff and students. Finally, all these variables must be expected to change over time and thus must be the subject of constant review and revision.

RESOURCES AND REFERENCES

It is difficult to suggest how one might become acquainted with the range of user needs. Perhaps the best way is to become a user. The paper by Austin of Harvard (1971) quoted in the text is certainly worth reading. Hunt (1971) reports a statistical analysis of user characteristics and their jobs at one university computer center. Schiffman (1970) reviews user needs from the point of view of the computer center management.

Orr (1968) presents a collection of papers intended as an exploration of the nature and importance of interactive computing. However, it also provides insight into the different ways one can use a computer and how computer use affects the problem-solving style of the user. Sackman (1970) is recommended here for much the same reason.

Beyond these sources one can only suggest that the reader talk to users or leaf through their articles. Books surveying computer use in different fields are numerous. Good bibliographies can be found in Blum (1970) and Levien (1972).

# 3

# ALTERNATIVE
# SOURCES OF
# COMPUTING

Outside of higher education, most computer installations tend to serve a homogeneous user community. All the applications in a bank, a government department, or an industrial laboratory usually have similar requirements, in terms of the dimensions described in Chapter Two. While a commercial service bureau or time-sharing company serves a heterogeneous community, its service is either moderately broad or moderately narrow, attracting those who find it satisfactory, while others look elsewhere. A company may not attract enough customers because its service is too limited, or because its service is so general that the price is too high for users with other options available to them.

Thus most computer centers serve a user community of one

or at most two groups of users. (Administrative functions may share a center with engineering applications, for example.) Academic computer users, on the other hand, encompass almost the entire range of possible requirements. Designing a service to suit them all is an unusually difficult task. The different attitudes and styles of administrators, faculty, and students combined with the different methods of the schools of science, engineering, business, and medicine stretch to the limits the service possible from a single organization. The computer center is expected to satisfy all these needs in depth, providing software, documentation, and knowledgeable consultants. This requirement is not appreciably less at smaller colleges than at large universities (although special users such as schools of law and medicine are fewer); yet the budget for these services at the small college is much lower.

Because of this requirement for breadth and depth, institutions have tended to provide multiple centers with more specialized services, or to combine their resources with other small institutions in order to maximize use and financial support, and to create a broad range of services. Paradoxically, neither of these alternatives has succeeded in dimming the popularity of the single, unified, on-campus computer center, for the users, diverse as they are, remain part of a single educational entity that seems to form a natural unit.

Presently computing services offer several radically different alternatives, which often leads to uneasy truces on campus: because one alternative accommodates some users better than others, it will have its advocates, but because the same alternative does not suit all the users, it will have its detractors. This chapter and the following one will describe some of these alternatives. The four basic modes are the campus computer center, distributed computing on campus, commercial services, and super centralization. Because each of these has its particular advantages and because each is the primary mode of service at a number of colleges and universities, I examine them in some detail.

CAMPUS COMPUTER CENTER

The case of the developent of computing at Exemplary College is not atypical. A group of professors becomes interested in using the computer in their reasearch and in making it available to their students. In addition, the comptroller wants computer access to start automating some of his procedures. Together, they bring this need to the attention of the president. Their proposal is quite straightforward, resembling that for any other expensive piece of capital equipment: it explains why computing is valuable and recommends buying a computer and locating it convenient to the major users.

This is a perfectly natural approach which has by and large been followed in business and industry in their use of computers. Because of the high cost and the rapid obsolescence of computers, many organizations have chosen to lease rather than buy them. Fewer educational institutions than commercial ones have taken this course, however, partly because they do not have the tax advantages that profit-making organizations do in leasing expensive equipment, and partly because they have preferred capital expenditures to long-term commitments to pay for a service. It is always easier to buy a solid object than to pay for an elusive service.

In the smaller college, or the large institution with a small group of users, the on-campus, college-directed computer center has some natural advantages. Since control resides with the users, they can arrange the rules to suit themselves, and access can be as easy or as difficult as they choose. To the college as a whole accrue the intangible benefits of showing prospective faculty and freshmen the computer room and of referring in the catalog to the College Computer Facility located in the basement of Old North. Finally, a very real consideration is that donors can be found for capital acquisitions more easily than for a few years of service from an off-campus agent. Imagine trying to convince an old grad to establish the Joe Smith Memorial Telephone Bill Fund! Computer service is not much different.

As the computing needs grow, the first computer at Exemplary College will be replaced by a larger one. Professional operators now man the machine and a manager is in charge of it—it has now become institutionalized and is beginning to move out of the grasp of the users who brought it onto the campus and who had such convenient and immediate access to it. At the same time, user needs begin to diverge and conflicts make it difficult for the users to share the same computer. Yet practical reasons exist for continuing to operate a campus computer center.

First, there is economy of scale in hardware. The unit cost of computation varies inversely with the size of the computer: if computer A has twice the size and power of computer B, a unit of computation will cost about half as much on A as on B (Grosch's Law). Thus considerably more computing can be bought for the same cost if the users pool their available funds. Second, some sophisticated applications can only be run on large computers. Large data bases, complex systems of simulation, information retrieval, or data analysis require the hardware resources of a large computer. Third, user services cannot economically be decentralized. If there are several smaller computers, each with its own procedures and software, where will users go for help when they are in trouble?

The first crack in the solidarity of the user community is bound to appear between the academic and the administrative users. In fact, at most institutions that use computing for both purposes, centers have developed independently in the two camps, with no thought of a unified service. The style of operation needed by the two groups is quite different: the administrative user needs security, reliability, predictability, while the style that makes the computing center a good learning center is totally different—it should be relaxed, free, with room for improvisation and experiment.

Yet no technical reasons exist for this dichotomy. There are no basic differences in hardware requirements, although they can be invented if necessary. As indicated above, a strong economic argument can be made against the separation of users into two camps, and service into two centers. Yet the reasons for the separation are often compelling. To keep the two groups working together in harmony requires considerable management skill. Since this skill is in shorter supply even than money on many campuses, the bifurcation is allowed to occur and to continue.

As the user community continues to grow and to diversify, further splits may occur. Some user groups may have enough power and financial resources to break away from the unified computing center. The medical school of a large university is likely to do so, for example. Also hard to coerce is a major scientific research project with government financing. It represents considerable power and may choose to go its own way. Finally, for reasons indicated in Chapter Two, the Computer Science Department may have its own small computer for conducting its more disruptive research.

The justification for these splits, as for the one between administrative and academic users, is essentially managerial and political, not economic. Grosch's Law continues to hold and cooperation continues to make computing cheaper. However, another rule of thumb applies to the economics of the case and mitigates somewhat the impartial application of Grosch's Law. Although the cost of computing *per se* is cheaper on a large computer, it is also true that generality is always more expensive than specialization. Grosch's Law pertains to hardware only, while this second rule applies to systems. Thus it may be more practical to build separate systems for the scientific users of large quantities of arithmetic computation and for the interactive user, in order to optimize each. Still, the major problems continue to be policy, control, and management, rather than hardware and economics. To many users, the advantages of size and power are less important than those of access and stability.

At one university where the business school has established its own computing center, the chief architect of the move was asked why. "If you use the campus computer center," he said, "you are always at the mercy of somebody else. They are going to change their systems and their machines. They will revise the schedule, alter the priorities, and raise the rates. You never know where you are going to stand six months from now. We own our machine, we control it, and we can use it in the way we think is most effective for our purposes."

As blocks of users withdraw their support from the campus center, the director and the administration are left in a quandary. The center has a large and expensive system of machines and personnel, a resource relatively fixed in cost. The most profitable business is moving away, leaving the center with important (but only marginally profitable) work and lots of idle time. A well-run large computer center can perform great quantities of work at a reasonable cost; it can serve student users with fast turnaround for their short jobs; it can provide exotic systems and experts who understand how to use them. But without the large users who supplied the bulk of the support, the computing center must operate at a deficit. And, if it is disbanded, who will serve the requirements of the student users and who will provide the services so important to many of the smaller users?

A few of the universities facing the problem of multiplying computing centers have tried to control the situation by giving a single individual on campus the responsibility for all the computing resources, or at least all those that provide services to more than a single user or project. He is likely to have a title equivalent to a dean or chief administrative officer. Because he is added after the fact, his position may remain that of staff to the top administration rather than in line control of the resources he must try to manage: while he can assume control of new acquisitions, he often has great difficulty in grasping control of existing redundant services.

The situation at one prominent university provides an example of the complexity of on-campus computing. The organization includes an associate provost for computing, assisted and guided by a university computing facilities committee. Reporting to the associate provost is the director of computation, who has responsibility for the operation of three of the university's largest computer centers: one general-purpose center, a research facility, and another in the medical school. However, the managers of these centers report both to him and to the heads of the enterprises their computers serve. Thus a gap is evident in the organization chart, with the troops dividing their loyalty between two sets of officers. Two other centers have not yet even come under the control of this official computing structure. The managers of these five major centers each have a user committee to assist in establishing policy. Beyond these five centers are the numerous smaller computers serving individual departments or research projects.

The complexity and confusion of this situation force the users to search for clarity and stability elsewhere, thus confusing the situation even further. A visitor to the campus hears this argument from users: "There are five computers I could use, with five procedures, five control languages, and five different rate structures. At least one of them is always in the process of changing. I never know where I stand; I don't have any influence over any of them. In my new NSF proposal, I am asking for funds to get my own computer."

A situation like this is clearly out of control. Restoring administrative control means wrenching power away from users and transferring it to the associate provost for computing, making him in fact what holders of such offices are often called in jest, "computer czar." Since such a move implies administrative preemption of faculty prerogatives, it clearly cannot be achieved without much difficulty.

Thus the campus computing center, begun as a pooling of interests with academic and economic justification, evolves into a labyrinth of power politics, complex schedules, plans, budgets, and managerial dispute. The innocent user is likely to feel very out of place indeed in this context. Computing has become big, expensive, and important on the campus—perhaps too big, too expensive, and too important for its own good or the good of the educational objectives it is designed to serve.

DISTRIBUTED COMPUTING

The recent development of economical small computers has abetted the revolt from the campus computing center. Although they would have been considered machines of substantial capabilities ten years ago, they are small by today's standards. Because of their modest physical size and nominal price, they have acquired the generic name "mini-computers." Many users with moderate amounts of computing ask whether they should spend their computing dollars for service from a general-purpose center or for mini-computers of their own. The answer depends, of course, on the nature and quality of service they are looking for. Comparing the mini-computer with a large model in terms of the characteristics discussed in Chapter Two, it is clear that the mini has superior response time, for no matter how good the response time of the campus center, the mini is always available. Predictability is also no problem on a mini. When the user has his own computer, he does not need to plan ahead when he will use it and for how long. The reliability of the mini-computers is quite high. Besides, in the case of the more popular ones, other machines that could be used in an emergency are probably available within a few miles. Security is easily assured: when the computer is locked up in the user's laboratory, it is as secure as any other resource he uses. Interaction is available: some mini-computers will support several interactive terminals simultaneously. If a user does not need this service, models are available without it, so that he can buy the computer that best suits his need, without paying for unneeded capabilities. Quantity is a problem, for here the mini is no match for the large computer if the work being planned demands fast computation in a large memory. Service level may also be a drawback on the mini. It comes with instruction manuals, but if the user needs professional help, he has to find it for himself. However, special hardware and software needs are more readily handled, since the user will shop around for the mini-computer that has what he needs in the way of both. Conversely, he does not need to convince an indifferent computer center manager or committee that they should invest in special devices and programs for him. Policy is also much simpler with a mini. The user controls the machine and runs it at his discretion. Finally, since the mini-computer is more specialized than the large machines, it can be adapted to suit the precise needs of the user. He does not pay (as he must in the campus computing center) for services and facilities of which he can make no use. Because the mini will be engineered to suit a smaller range of tasks, it may even be easier to use. "The trouble with the large centers," one mini user explains, "is that they are engineered to do a large number of complicated jobs; but there is no way to do simple jobs on them anymore."

Certainly the mini-computer appears to have many advantages over the centralized service. Thus the concept of total decentralization emerges: let individual projects or small groups of users acquire the computer that best suits their needs, dispensing completely with the central computer facility. Instead of the general-purpose facility, the hardware, software, and policy for each computer can be suited to the specialized requirements of a much smaller user community. However, this decentralized environment, ideal for some users, can be disastrous for others. A decentralized computing situation lacks facilities for the user who needs a great *quantity* of computing, but only part of the time—he has to have a small portion of a large facility. Also, the user who needs the service of consultants and software experts cannot be served by a computer in a closet. Finally, the person who wants a small amount of computing service for a limited period of time has no place to go.

It is also questionable whether the economy of the institution as a whole, as opposed to that of individual users, is served. The user's estimate of economy is probably based on his guess as to the peak load of work his project will generate. When he is not loading the machine to capacity, it is idle, for he has no convenient way to dispose of computing he does not need. He may give it away or even sell it to another project at a discount, thus further undermining the financial position of the campus computing center, with which he is now in competition.

If the three classes of users who cannot be satisfied with min-computers are to have some vehicle, the central computing facility must be protected. At various universities, ingenious schemes are being devised to structure and control the mini-computer invasion. A research project at the University of California at Irvine is investigating a "Distributed Computing System," which would draw a number of small computers into a ring network. Users would submit their jobs, which would be passed around the ring until they were accepted by some computer with the time and facility to perform them. Several other universities are developing schemes in which the mini-computers are linked to the central facility in some way: small jobs are run on the mini-computer and larger jobs or overload are forwarded to the campus center. In no case has it been seriously proposed that users be forbidden from acquiring the little machines that are causing all the trouble.

COMMERCIAL SERVICE

If the on-campus center is not able to provide the type and level of service the user wants and if a user-managed mini-computer is not the answer for one reason or another, a third alternative exists: buy the service from some off-campus agency. Many industrial corporations and banks are willing to sell their unneeded computing capacity. Other organizations sell computing and computer-related services as their primary product. The advantages in acquiring computing in this way are several: usually, when buying service from a commercial agency, the user need not make the long-range commitment implicit in buying or leasing equipment and hiring personnel; at least in some parts of the country, a range of alternative services is available, allowing the user to select the one that best suits his needs; and finally, the buyer exercises the kind of leverage buyers have always had: the right to take their business elsewhere. This may not affect a business that is just unloading unwanted computer time. But if the company's major business is selling computing services, it is very much aware of a need to satisfy its customers.

TYPICAL CASES

The following examples are typical of many colleges that choose this route for some or all of their computing services.

College W is a small liberal arts institution with no on-campus computer. For reasons of economy, they have contracted with their bank for some data processing services: payroll preparation, accounts receivable, and so on. They send the inputs to the bank and get back standardized reports; they have nothing to do with the computer themselves and employ no computer programmers or analysts.

College X has a computer center for administrative and academic users. However, since it cannot supply the interactive service for which a strong demand exists, interactive computing is purchased from a local time-sharing company for those applications requiring it.

At college Y, Professor Jones of the business school wants to use Simscript, a language especially developed for the writing of simulation programs. Sufficient interest does not exist to justify installing it on the system in the campus facility, so the college contracts with an off-campus agency for service, including software, hardware, and a Simscript expert to help out if Professor Jones gets into difficulties.

The administration at the University of Z wants to develop an integrated and inclusive information system for maintaining financial, personnel, facility, and student records. It will mean a considerable investment in preparing the programs. Not having the personnel and being unable to hire qualified programmers for a one-year effort, they contract with a software company for personnel services to produce the programs they need.

All these examples indicate how an institution can supplement its other resources with the purchase of computer-related services for special purposes. Should a college consider acquiring all its computing in this way? The notion cannot be rejected out of hand. It relieves administrators of many burdens, principally that of managing a group of technicians whose work they do not understand very well and of making heavy long-range financial commitments.

Still, buying computer service seems to make many people uncomfortable. In an NSF-funded study by the Southern Regional Education Board, for example, various computing services were supplied to a group of small colleges. Those who used a time-shared service from a commercial agency were convinced of the value of computing, but not necessarily of buying only the service: after the experiment, several of the colleges cancelled the commercial service and leased or purchased a small computer for on-campus installation.

The computing director at one large university confesses that according to his analysis, the university computing needs can be met at about the same price from leased or purchased equipment and from commercial services. Since no clear-cut advantage could be found either way, this university decided to purchase its own computer as the "safest" way to go.

CUSTOM-MADE VENDOR

Few large institutions will find vendors of computing services large enough to satisfy all their needs. Case-Western Reserve University invented a solution to this problem by setting up an independent, wholly university-owned, for-profit corporation and becoming its first customer. The long-term computing contract with the university enabled the new company, the Chi Corporation, to get a bank loan sufficient to acquire the necessary equipment. After several years of operation, the university is still Chi's largest customer, but it is not its only one. Chi now has over 350 customers.

Chi has inspired several other similar developments. The Alpha Corporation of Southern Methodist University, for instance, is located on the campus and operated by university personnel. Although independent, it looks like a university computer center. By contrast, the intent of the Case-Western Reserve effort was to make Chi really independent of its sponsor so that it would ultimately not look or behave like an arm of the university to other potential customers.

The feasibility of such an alternative demands a considerable user base: at least one-half to one million dollars of computing service a year, and more managerial adroitness than many universities can muster. In the words of one observer, it is also necessary to overcome carefully and patiently "the unbelievable insularity of higher educational institutions."

At Harvard, the university's strong tradition of decentralization and minimum university-wide services or control has made it particularly difficult to create and manage a centralized computing facility there. Yet the problems it has faced are not so unusual as to make its experiences irrelevent to other institutions. In 1970, much of the campus computing was being supplied by mini-computers and other specialized centers, all of the interactive service was being obtained from commercial sources or other universities, and the university-wide computer center, which supplied batch service to those who wished to use it, was displaying a considerable deficit. With no promise of any significant growth in the use of this facility in the foreseeable future, some major changes seemed called for. On-going commitments prevented shutting the center down altogether; nor was it possible to compel more users to keep their computing dollars on campus—yet the university was not willing to continue underwriting the computing deficit.

In the face of this dilemma, Harvard decided to share a common computing facility with its close neighbor, MIT. A single center would serve as a central facility on both campuses. It would be located at MIT but the management, operation, control, and use would be shared by the two institutions as equal partners. The Harvard computing center would contain equipment to communicate with MIT rather than to process the work on site. This shared facility was set up with the agreement (which might well terrify most sensible administrators) that the details of management would be worked out only after the system was operational and personnel on both campuses had had some experience in using it.

In the summer of 1972, after one year of operation, several facts were clear. First, the interests of the two partners were not the same. MIT foresaw a continued growth in their use of the facility and was prepared to expand its batch capability and add a time-sharing capability. Harvard, on the other hand, foresaw its use of the facility remaining at a fairly constant level, because so much of its computing was being supplied from other sources. Further, after its experience with computing deficits, Harvard wanted to keep its commitment to future computing costs as low and as short-range as possible. Yet the partnership in that first year had been an unqualified technical and financial success: service had been continuous and good, and deficits had been sharply reduced at both institutions. In the light of such success, Harvard decided to withdraw from the partnership, becoming instead a customer of MIT for computing services. By adjusting its contract to meet its needs and by paying a fixed price to MIT, Harvard will obtain the same level of service, but remain free of any long-term commitment. MIT, on the other hand, will be free to expand the service and manage it to suit its own needs. Thus both institutions have attained some of the advantages of the alternatives described in this chapter.

SUPERCENTRALIZATION

In addition to the mini invasion and the advance of commercial agencies, another form of computing has arisen to threaten the stability and question the wisdom of the on-campus computer center: cooperative or regional ventures for supplying computing for educational purposes. The reasons for the emergence of this concept are not hard to find. If centralization at the campus level has advantages, intercampus centralization may be better yet: greater economies of scale should appear; requirements for unusual or very large systems could be pooled among several institutions; the load on under- or over-utilized computers could be more rationally distributed; and limited personnel resources could be stretched to maximum usefulness. In 1968 arguments like these convinced the National Science Foundation to fund a few experimental networks in which a single center provided computing services to several campuses. Encouraged by the initial success of these, NSF funded more of them, for a total of about thirty. Although not all of these supercenters have been successful, many have survived and others are still being organized. They promise to change considerably the way in which at least part of the computing needed for higher education is provided. The following chapter explores in some detail the technical and managerial problems that they present.

RESOURCES AND REFERENCES

A good introduction to the range of alternatives and some of the issues relevant to deciding between them is found in the report of a 1971 meeting of EDUCOM, the Interuniversity Communications Council (*The Financing and Organization of Computing in Higher Education,* 1971). In particular, the discussion summaries reflect some rather heated debate between proponents of minicomputers and regional networks. Descriptions of the Chi and Alpha Corporations are also included in this volume.

Information on the characteristics of the various computers currently on the market is found in *Computer Characteristics Review,* a periodical catalog, or the "Computer Directory and Buyer's Guide" that appears annually in the monthly magazine *Computers and Automation.* A good introduction to mini-computers and their applicability to educational purposes will be found in Osborne (1971). Knights (1970) deals more specifically with mini-computers in research use. Theis and Hobbs (1971) is a survey with tabular information on available minis; in a second article (1970) they present a similar analysis of available terminals. However, the small computer market is so rapidly changing that the reader may want to find more up-to-date material. *Datamation,* the magazine that published these two surveys, may publish later revisions to them. In addition, a general bibliographic source like *Computing Reviews* can be used to locate recent and topical information on this or any other computer-related subject.

Although not written specifically for the academic environment, Ray (1970) on service bureaus is of interest to those considering commercial sources of service. Schwab (1968) may also have some useful data, although it was written with commercial organizations in mind. DeGabrielle (1971) briefly describes some of the advantages of commercial service for student use. Further references to the shared use of computers are at the end of Chapter Four.

The publications and other services of several organizations are of considerable interest. The Special Interest Group on University Computer Centers (SIGUCC) of the Association for Computing Machinery publishes a newsletter and holds periodic meetings. It is primarily an association of computing center directors and its interests reflect the current problems of this group. EDUCOM, one of whose reports has already been recommended, does consulting, gives seminars, and holds biannual meetings. The meetings and the published reports of them are excellent introductions to the problems of computing from the point of view of the top administration, in contrast to the more technical orientation of the computing center director. Originally an association of large universities, the organization has recently begun to display a greater interest in the problems of the smaller colleges. EDUCOM's publications also include a quarterly bulletin that contains general information about activity in the computer world and also more substantial articles.

# 4

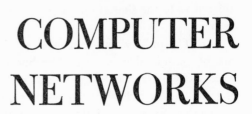

# COMPUTER NETWORKS

The most noticeable characteristic of computer networks seems to be their variety of form—no two are administered exactly alike. Three general classes may be distinguished, however: a network of one large institution which houses the computer center and a number of smaller colleges; a network of both large (at least two) and small (any number can play) institutions, with the computer center on neutral ground and organizationally independent; a network that has more than a single source of service, at least two of the nodes on the network offer (as well as use) computing services. The first two networks are usually called "star" networks because they have a single center to which all the other nodes are connected, so that a diagram of its organization resembles a sunburst or star. Networks of the third type are more complex; I call them distributed networks, because providers as well as users of service are distributed in a complex fashion.

UNIVERSITY-CENTERED STAR NETWORK

A decade ago, when computing was a relative novelty, several small colleges located within a few miles of one another would often discuss pooling their resources to create a single computing center. Such discussions were usually frustrating affairs. The requirement that small colleges make sizeable financial commitments for long-term collaboration on a highly technical matter was too much for most of them to accept. It seemed necessary that a single institution accept the burden and the risk of estimating requirements and supplying the resource. A large host institution could absorb the bulk of the service and expense, while supplying a range of service broad enough to fill the needs of the smaller institutions. In an association of a large university and several small colleges, the computing center could treat its off-campus customers simply as additional departments of its own host. Little in the way of special treatment would be needed. Most of the networks that developed in the 1960s followed this pattern. The University of Iowa, Oregon State, and Dartmouth are good examples; the numerous unsuccessful ones are better left unlisted.

One of these anonyous failures was formed around a large university that had just installed a computer large enough to allow for anticipated growth over the next several years. It offered interactive service to local colleges and high schools, and was able to get a three-year grant from NSF to pay a large share of the costs. During these three years the colleges and high schools got some free computing, which allowed them to experiment and decide for themselves on the value of these services for their institutions. The grant also allowed the university to sell its excess capacity and avoid a possible deficit. After the three years, the partnership ended. The computing needs of the university had increased enough to absorb most of its computing resources; the colleges and high schools found the services from the university to be overpriced and unresponsive to their needs.

In a case like this, if the requirements of the small institution are a subset of those of the university users, they can be satisfied. But if the small college needs a special service not required by university users, it is likely to find itself ignored, with little to use in the way of leverage or influence. And, as the sophistication of the small user increases, his demands for more complex service will not be able to compete with the supplier's on-campus research projects and academic departments.

Not all star networks are this unresponsive. Dartmouth College developed an early successful experimental system which offered its on-campus customers time-shared interactive computing. This innovation encouraged the appearance of interesting and valuable instructional materials in many disciplines and using different pedagogical techniques. With NSF help the system was expanded and offered to other colleges, at many of which it has been found very valuable, for the range of services, especially in software and instructional materials, is greater than could be acquired by any other means.

The Middle Atlantic Education and Research Center (MERC) is a group of smaller institutions which formed a cooperative regional computing organization. After NSF financial support terminated, the member colleges had to accept financial responsibility for the computer facility. By this time, however, the colleges were also feeling the financial pinch of the times and found it difficult to commit themselves to cooperation and long-term financial obligation. Consequently, the largest member institution, Franklin and Marshall College, assumed responsibility for the planning and financing of the center, selling its services to the other members of the corporation and other subscribers. Thus an originally innovative organizational plan degenerated into a conventional star network.

The network that offers service to unsophisticated users is selling a product to a purchaser who often has little skill in evaluating what he is being offered. When the director of the computer center at the state university visits the mathematics professor at a small liberal arts college in order to offer him computing services, the situation is not unlike the classic image of the used car salesman and the little old lady. The seller must exercise some restraint and acknowledge some moral obligation in this environment. He should be sure that his system will work: the customer colleges should not be expected to pay for the privilege of debugging the university's system. If the college is paying the full price for the service it is getting, it must be treated as a first-class customer, receiving the same consideration as an on-campus user. The university administration must be aware that the cost of documenting the system for remote use, acquiring and coordinating hardware, software, and communications, marketing the service to potential customers, and servicing these users once they are acquired will take a great deal of time and effort on the part of university personnel; this is time that cannot be spent dealing with on-campus problems.

Both the buyer and seller must be aware that, despite the number of such systems that have been created, technical problems of considerable magnitude may be encountered. The college may have a small computer on its campus which will perform some initial processing on a job and then forward it via telephone lines to the central processor at the university. When the system does not work (particularly when it is first installed), locating the difficulty is a complex problem, requiring a highly skilled expert. The trouble may be in the programs in one computer or the other; it may be in one of the pieces of hardware (probably of different manufacturers) located at either of the sites; it may be in the telephone service being provided by one of the two or three companies through whose areas the lines pass. Someone is responsible for the proper operation of each of these components, but until the finger is pointed at the specific element that is failing, little will be done.

### INDEPENDENT STAR NETWORK

A second, relatively rare structure is like the first, but lacks a university at the center. The only totally successful model is the Triangle Universities Computation Center (TUCC) in North Carolina. Three large universities in the same vicinity set up this organization as an independent corporation owned by the universities. Established with the aid of NSF, TUCC is now self-supporting, supplying the bulk of the computing used by North Carolina at Chapel Hill, North Carolina State at Raleigh, and Duke at Durham. Computing is also sold to a state agency, the North Carolina Educational Computing Service, which in turn retails the service to many smaller public and private institutions throughout the state. None of the three universities has all its computing done by TUCC, but all three buy the largest share of their computing from it.

It is hard to isolate the one or two critical factors that would have to be duplicated if the success of TUCC were to be transported to another area. Several elements seem important: the three universities are similar enough in size to prevent one from dominating the other two in a joint effort; their geographic proximity allows for frequent face-to-face meetings at several levels of administration; there was also a small but growing tradition of interinstitutional cooperation that TUCC could build on. Finally, TUCC has clearly captured the interest, enthusiasm, and trust of many of the users and of the state legislature. Since most of its funding comes indirectly from the state via the two state institutions that are members, the interest of the state government is a strong factor in its survival.

The Chancellor's Office of the California State University and Colleges coordinates a group of nineteen institutions, ranging from moderately small to very large. Like many such offices, it quickly realized the frightening cost of providing uncoordinated computing service to its member institutions. It therefore produced a plan whereby the colleges could acquire the computing they needed on a structured and hopefully economical basis. Each of the campuses in this plan has some computing capability of its own (as do the computing centers of the three North Carolina universities in the previous example), with teleprocessing capabilities that allow them to send jobs beyond their limited capacities to one of the two super-centers that were created for this purpose. These centers can communicate with one another and send work back and forth to balance loads. In addition, they can send work to an even larger and more sophisticated center outside the network. This center (UCLA's on-campus facility) provides bulk computing for very large jobs plus many of the more specialized software systems of interest to only a few users on the California State campuses.

The California State system is not universally beloved by all its users. Many argue that the tight control it imposes on its members restrains growth, innovation, and worthwhile independent investigation. But it is hard to believe that this argument will carry the day. The leaders in computer application may have been restrained by being harnessed into this system, but the followers have been prodded along by being coupled with them. The system has the ordered symmetry that bureaucrats and legislators admire. More education is probably bought relative to the computing dollars spent than could be approached by any other alternative. It is also worth noting here that the California system is the only one of those cited that was constructed entirely with state funds, without any support from the National Science Foundation.

The New Jersey Office of Computer Planning and Information Systems was established by the state's board of higher education in an effort to improve the calibre of computing service at the state colleges and universities. A study was conducted which culminated in the receipt of an NSF grant and the creation of the New Jersey Educational Computer Center Corporation. This organization established its own computer support facility and also purchased computing from the two large universities in the state (one public and one private), acting as a broker in supplying this power to smaller institutions.

In this case, too, success is clearly due to effort at the state level, where a government agency took the initiative in providing convenient computing to the colleges of New Jersey. Continued success seems likely, unless the state loses confidence in it, or unless the colleges prove that another model can provide them with better resources at a lower price.

### DISTRIBUTED NETWORK

A third alternative differs markedly from the first two. In the star networks the nodes at the periphery are customers, while the one at the center is the source of the computing services. A distributed network, by contrast, has multiple sources of service. Suppose that several institutions have computing centers offering services that do not totally overlap: some of the services are available at each center, but others are available only at one. The academic users at all of the campuses would have a wider range of resources if the facilities were linked together into a network so that the user had equal access to any of the centers.

In New England, a number of institutions invite other colleges to use their computive services. NERCOMP (New England Regional Computing Program) was organized to facilitate access by its members to any of six such systems. While NERCOMP itself does not control any of the computers, it links the centers together by leasing telephone lines, and providing the mechanisms for using colleges to share these lines at a reasonable cost. It has established standards of documentation, enabling users to learn how to gain access to the systems on the network; and it also distributes this documentation. At last count, 42 colleges and universities in New England were members of NERCOMP, using it to supply some or all of their computing needs.

A somewhat different kind of distributed network is represented by MERIT, a system that links the computing facilities of the University of Michigan, Michigan State, and Wayne State. With the computers linked by telephone lines, a user can submit at his local center a job that is destined for any of the three computers. A special feature of the system is that it allows a program on one computer to initiate a job on another, thus enabling the user to construct complex processes involving the use of more than a single machine. For most users, however, the attraction of such a system is bound to reside in the software and systems that are not available at his local computer, but are accessible at a remote site with equal convenience.

Since other nation-wide networks are being planned which will have the centerless characteristics of MERIT, the Michigan network deserves close observation. Its problems and its success or failure in solving them will be an indication of the difficulties facing other such nets. Technical problems certainly exist in great number, along with a novel managerial problem: managers of computing centers must try to operate a growing business in an era of decreasing research expenditures and shrinking educational budgets. They may see the network as an opportunity for work and money to flow into their facilities. If other members of the network are interested in paying to have work done (as in a successful star network), a community of interest exists. But a community of agents, all of whom have something to sell and no money to buy, cannot agree on common interests. One cannot have a network of sellers alone.

NETWORK AND USER

The use of such a network can offer some considerable advantages to the smaller college. Assuming minimum charges for communications, it is the most economical selection possible for very small amounts of computing. Another advantage is that the long-range commitments are minimal, making it very attractive to institutions where computing is still an experiment and not a commitment.

The college that joins a regional consortium joins a group of relatively knowledgeable and sophisticated users who can teach the faculty, students, and staff of the new college much about large modern systems, software, and methods. Instead of learning modern computer methods by trial and error, as would be the case if they purchased their own small machine, the new users are likely to be brought up quickly to a high level of knowledge.

All the arrangements described above imply the ready availability of user services, not just access to a large and powerful computer. Some of the more successful centers bear this out. The history of the University of Iowa Regional Computer Network reveals that exchange of information by all possible means figured prominently in the planning and organization of the network. A board of curriculum experts, full-time campus coordinators at each participating college, emphasis on travel for face-to-face contact, workshops and seminars, and ample technical assistance to the colleges from the university all played a large part in the network's success.

In North Carolina, the Educational Computing Service, based on the TUCC computer, reaches public and private institutions throughout the state. Retailing services as ECS does is not just a matter of marketing and sending bills; it consists also of packaging the commodity in a form useful to the potential customer. ECS has devoted its attentions largely to the creation, encouragement, and distribution of instructional software. They can offer a college a large collection of instructional materials in many disciplines, all of which incidentally require computing that can be obtained from

TUCC via ECS. What attracts potential users are the application programs (both batch and interactive) that students can use, the documentation and personnel support that helps with their use, and finally readily available computing.

Another important advantage of large centers which serve many users is that they can support many useful software systems that would be too expensive and too little used in the context of a smaller user community. The California State network is linked to the UCLA computer facility largely because UCLA retains one of the largest libraries of programs and systems available anywhere. All of the nineteen campuses of the California State system have access to this library for a fraction of what it would cost the campuses to maintain the library independently.

Even in the matter of hardware a range of alternatives exists. Centers like Dartmouth and Oregon offer interactive service by means of typewriter-like terminals that are ideal for the instructional uses on which these systems focus, but less desirable for research and other instructional applications. The Iowa and California networks are oriented primarily to batch rather than interactive service, with small computers on the campuses acting as remote input-output stations to the central computers. At the other end of the spectrum, TUCC provides its services to its three member universities via the fairly large-scale computers on their campuses.

The enthusiasm of those who have worked successfully in the regional centers runs so high that they sometimes believe alternative points of view are unsupportable. The super-center certainly represents an exciting alternative with many advantages, but it is equally clear that it is not the solution to everyone's problem.

James Farmer, of the California State University and Colleges and one of the principal architects of their network, points out that in many cases, economics do not favor the very large machine in the academic environment. The large computer requires a high and steady load that is inconsistent with the seasonal nature of student jobs, which begin slowly at the onset of the semester, peak just before final examinations, and then drop to zero. Also, for this kind of job, the overhead of the complex operating system of the large center may be excessive. Thus, for sheer economy (leaving power, sophistication, and user services out of the argument), the medium-size machine may be a better choice.

Then, too, the managerial issues cannot always be solved to the users' satisfaction. One college president, with experience in on-campus as well as off-campus computing says, "What is needed is a service-oriented organization, with merchandising skills. And most academic centers are just not oriented that way. The conflict between internal and external demand is a tougher problem than most computing center directors are equipped to deal with."

In several states ambitious plans are being formulated for a totally integrated, state-wide computer network for higher education. The Illinois plan, for example, considers the needs of private and community colleges as well as state institutions. In Florida, a centralized system for administrative purposes has been established. However, plans to extend this to academic users have been postponed or discarded for a variety of reasons. An early decision was made to pursue a centralized "computer utility" for all campuses of the University of Wisconsin. The plan was later abandoned because of technical and managerial problems, the latter caused largely by intercampus rivalries. Significantly, the Wisconsin effort, like others at that time, originated with the computing director at the main campus (Madison), a level at which the problems of intercampus relationships could not be easily dealt with. Later efforts, such as the one in Illinois, are being instigated at the level of state boards of higher education, where the managerial problems can be treated more effectively.

The open or tacit decision to back away from the management problems of interinstitutional cooperative computing is not necessarily an expression of timidity in the face of difficulties. It may proceed from a realistic appraisal of the administration's capabilities and priorities. At one private university a visitor reminded a vice-president that better management would solve the financial crisis in the computing center. He smiled painfully and said, "Computing is a two-million-dollar headache, you are right. But the university as a whole has a twenty-million-dollar headache. Which would you have us tackle first?"

Finally, there is the difficulty of cultivating interinstitutional cooperation in any but the most trivial affairs. Commenting on problems of network development, Gerard Weeg of the University of Iowa wrote, "Logic is one thing and incentive is another." External pressure is sometimes needed to make a college accept off-campus computing, even when it is the logical choice. Even when this alternative is not the most economical or efficient, external force may be applied, simply because some government agency cannot tolerate the disorganization, lack of control, and financial complexity of decentralized computing.

## NATIONAL NETWORKS

One further alternative, that of national cooperation, is now in the experimental stage. Its supporters argue that among research users, hardware, software, and personnel are discipline-dependent, not geographic. A geologist from Maine, for instance, needs the same kinds of computer languages, the informational data bases, the simulations and the knowledgeable consultants that the geologist in South Dakota or Hawaii needs. He has more in common with his colleagues in his discipline than with his colleagues on the Maine campus. Might not the best and most effective source of computing for him be a national center for geological information services? The communications costs in such a system are bound to be high but they may be outweighed by the economies of specialization at the center and by the greater efficiency possible to the users.

The case is not really as clear as this argument suggests, and discussions and studies proceed. Should needs really be isolated in a discipline-oriented fashion and if so, how should subdisciplines be combined? Perhaps it would be more efficient to cluster all number-crunching applications in one center, and all data-base management applications in another.

Some national discipline-oriented centers now exist, but as sources of computing services they have assumed only minor importance so far. The Inter-university Consortium for Political Research (ICPR) at Michigan does not offer computing as such to its members but it does supply some closely related services, including advice to political scientists on selecting and using the facilities available to them, and maintenance and distribution (for a fee) of a data management system (OSIRIS II). Also, an important function of the consortium is the maintenance in machine-readable form of an extensive archive of political science data, from which members may request copies.

The National Bureau of Economic Research is developing software for economics. It will not operate a service facility but will install its programs at facilities where interested users may gain access to them. It appears that the bureau will select one or two facilities to act as national centers. Unlike ICPR, it will not distribute data or programs. Rather, it expects users to go where the information services exist, thus approaching more closely the model of a national discipline-oriented computing center.

The National Center for Atmospheric Research at Boulder has a very large computer which is available to research projects in the field that can demonstrate a need for use of the facility. The center provides special input and output devices, relatively good service, and is totally subsidized by NSF. Unlike most discipline-oriented centers, however, it does not appear to have any special software. A further limitation is that it is really only available to users who can come to Boulder to use it, since the center has no remote-access hardware and center policy does not allow service by mail. As a consequence, many users debug their programs on their own campuses and go to Boulder only for the lengthy and expensive production runs of their programs.

The Health Sciences Computer Facility at UCLA and a number of centers funded by the Atomic Energy Commission follow a similar pattern, providing free computing to those projects that can demonstrate their value and relevance to the goals of the centers. Serious consideration is also being given to a national center for computing in chemistry. However, until the number of such centers increases and their convenience is considerably improved, they do not promise to make serious inroads on the campus computing scene.

A vehicle for making a large number of centers as convenient to a user as his on-campus facility would be a national computer network. In the interest of furthering scientific research, the Department of Defense Advanced Research Products Agency (ARPA) has established a network that will allow the computers at any member center to communicate with those at any other. This ARPA network is the ultimate in interinstitutional cooperation for computing and already exists in experimental form. The hope is that the network will prove useful enough to become self-supporting, allowing it to leave its parent agency and sever its connection with the Department of Defense.

All of the current members of the ARPA network are universities and research centers. Ideally, a research user at any node selects from among all other nodes the one that best suits the needs of his current problem. He then submits the job to his local center, where the local computer transfers the job to the "interface message processor" (IMP), which in turn breaks the job down into a series of messages that are transferred from one IMP to the next across the country until the messages reach the site at which the user intends the job to be processed. There it is switched to the target computer and processed. The output is returned in the same fashion. To the user, the computer at his campus center thus becomes a link with all the other major sources of research computation in the United States and perhaps even beyond.

The key link in this chain, the IMP, is a special-purpose computer that costs about $45,000. To join the network, an institution must acquire an IMP and make the changes in its own hardware and software that are necessary to accommodate the system. Thereafter communication costs and maintenance must be paid; the user must also pay for the computer time he uses, wherever he uses it. Thus the expanded resources of this network do not come cheaply; the total cost runs about $30,000 a year, independent of the computer time used. Although the picture may change, the ARPA network is currently clearly a vehicle for large and expensive research applications—only major universities can afford membership in the club.

Of course, indirect use of the network is not impossible. A user at one of California's state colleges, for example, might submit a job to his campus center, where it would be transferred to the central computer of the California state college system in Los Angeles. From there it might be directed to UCLA, which is part of the California network and also of ARPA. However, the difficulties of negotiating this tortuous path would be likely to deter all but the hardiest and most determined scholar.

In 1972, NSF announced its interest in a national network to serve instructional as well as research users. As the plans for this "National Science Network" develop, more colleges may become involved. In its original announcement, however, NSF left the details of network structure open to specification by the academic community. It is thus too early to comment on the form this network may ultimately take.

### CONCLUSION

I have explained how the beleaguered on-campus computer center is threatened by both larger and smaller organizations. Good reasons exist for preferring both less and more organization in supplying computing for campus research, instructional, and administrative users. Since these users are no longer (if they ever truly were) homogeneous, a single campus may have sets of users which, if not totally incompatible, at least represent needs in serious conflict and make the simultaneous servicing of all of them a complex and expensive task. At one end of the spectrum, the mini-computer offers a high degree of individual control, but is best adapted to special applications and a limited set of services. At the regional or national level, the super-center can present a wider range of more unusual services, but the user has very little control over the management or accessibility of these resources. In between, the medium-sized campus computer offers a moderate amount of control and a good range of services. Thus all three are likely to remain as active and competing alternatives.

Campus computing center directors, however, will probably find little comfort in knowing that facilities like theirs will continue to exist for a while at some institutions. It is probably still true that every college needs a computing center, but that term may come to mean a locus for service rather than hardware. At small colleges, the center may not even provide the services it recommends and supports—the consultant's office may be backed up by a telephone line instead of a computer. At other institutions, the computing center's personnel, seeking to retain some useful role and seeing the advantages of becoming either very large or very specialized, may offer service well beyond the needs of their on-campus users. It may be that there will no longer be room for the medium-size, general-purpose, poorly managed computer center in the back of the engineering building. The center will have to attract business, either by being very economical or by offering some special service, such as an information management system and data base in a few selected disciplines, or an on-line system for some administrative function. In the long run, the campus computing center is bound to become more a well-run business closely associated with the college than an innovative instructional enterprise.

RESOURCES AND REFERENCES

A good brief introduction to the subject of regional networks for higher education is found in Weeg (1971). *Networks for Higher Education* (1972), another EDUCOM report, is a good survey. Its papers and discussion summaries go into many of the subjects presented in this chapter, especially the ARPA and NSF networks. In addition, it treats many of the implications of networks for special classes of users, libraries and medical schools, for instance. A special issue of *Datamation* (April 1972) contains several excellent papers on technical and managerial problems of networks, although not specifically educational networks. Parkhill (1966) contains detailed analyses of the implications of computing independent of geography. Duggan (1970) reports on yet another EDUCOM conference. De-Grasse (1971) is a pamphlet that reports a more recent survey; it contains a fair analysis of the promise and problem represented by networks. Like many of the references included here, it contains much more information on the technical aspects of network design and operation than I have included in my text.

Any number of comparative analyses of existing networks and regional centers have been made, most of them as a result of NSF grants. I have read quite a few of them and find it difficult to recommend any of them. Systems are described in terms of glowing admiration, while the weaknesses and very real problems of many networks are largely ignored. No one wants to document failures, I suppose; but a document that describes with admiration an enterprise that collapses of its own weight before the ink is dry deserves some scepticism. The EDUCOM report *Financing and Organization of Computing in Higher Education* (1971) does contain some useful descriptions; perhaps because the document is based on transcripts of conversations rather than on prepared text, it contains some straightforward description of real problems.

Those interested in more detailed information on ARPA are referred to reports presented at several national computer conferences. "Resource Sharing Computer Networks" (1970), "The ARPA Network" (1972), and McQuillan and others (1972) are probably the best sources commonly available, although people close to the network may have unpublished papers that are more current or more specific to a particular area of interest.

Other networks, too, are often best described in unpublished papers that are prepared for interested visitors, or in brochures that are distributed as long as they last. Much of my description is based on such ephemeral material. I have included in the bibliography, however, a paper on the TUCC network (Williams, 1972) and a series of papers on different aspects of the Dartmouth system ("The Dartmouth System and its Applications," 1969).

# 5

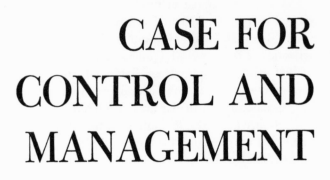

# CASE FOR
# CONTROL AND
# MANAGEMENT

At all but a few universities the top administrators, the president, provost, and vice-presidents, have usually devoted little attention to computing affairs. Only in a crisis that threatens the well-being of the college have the president and his closest associates stepped in to restore order. At most institutions, most of the time, the administration has had little reason to take the matter any more seriously than this. Until recently, funded research projects have ordinarily paid the lion's share of the computing bill; the rest was justifiable as an administrative expense or as an experimental teaching tool. The most the president could ask was that the political crises remain rare and require little of his attention and that the cost of keeping the computer not become too large a lump in the budget. In fact, if it could be hidden altogether, so much the better.

The manager of computing is usually pleased to comply with these requests. Attracting the minimum of attention from the president's office and from budget readers, in other words, "maintaining a low profile," means that the director is free to manage the affairs of computing as he sees fit, with little interference. So the president and the computing center director are both satisfied, and only the faculty, administrative staff, and students are sometimes frustrated in attempting to use the computer. And, at least until fairly recently, few of them knew enough about computing to be aware that better management might make the computer more useful to them.

At numerous such institutions, the attention of the president is captured only when the computer deficit grows too large to be hidden any longer. Dwindling research dollars and soaring costs make administrators wonder whether it is really necessary to invest so much in computing and whether, if budgets have to be cut, this may not be a very good place to start. So the president decides to apply a little management to the computing center. Besides, no matter what it costs, efficiently managed computing is computing that helps make good education and research happen, while badly managed computing is simply a drain on financial and other resources, even if the machine was purchased at a discount and is busy all the time. With good management, the resources should serve the needs of the institution effectively.

In the early days of computers, emphasis was naturally placed on the technology itself and the techniques of management lagged behind. Doing any work at all with a computer was in the nature of an adventure and an experiment. But it is now time for the management of computer use to catch up. When presented with a recommendation for expenditures for more classroom space or athletic equipment, most college presidents know how to ask the right questions and reach a decision on whether these investments would serve the best interests of the college. However, when the subject of the recommendation is computing, his lack of technical experience and unfamiliarity with the jargon sometimes prevent his asking the questions. And certainly, if he does not, no one will.

Consider the case at one large state university: the president received a recommendation from a blue ribbon committee to double
the computer center budget and acquire a complement of new
equipment which would quadruple the administrative and academic
computing capacity of the campus. Most of the argument supporting the recommendation was devoted to a careful comparison of the
proposals that had been received from six hardware vendors and a
justification for the selection of brand X. The committee that prepared the report had worked hard, and the members were proud
of their accomplishment; yet the president was incapable of understanding the technical details of the report and felt unsure about his
ability to persuade the legislature of the need for several hundred
thousands of dollars in additional computing funds. When he asked
members of the committee for explanations, the discussion bogged
down in throughput, cycles, benchmarks, and bits. The committee
was restive because, despite their explanations, the president would
not act on their recommendations.

A visitor to the campus, observing this stalemate, was able
to point out the root of the problem, too obvious for any of the
participants to have seen: no one was trying to bridge the gap
between the technical facts and the educational need. A college
president has no business being interested in the kind of information
that this president's advisory committee wanted him to judge. He
wanted to know (but, bewildered by the technicalities, did not ask)
what four times as much computing would do for his university,
and how it would make education, research, and administration
better. Once this fact was pointed out, the president was able to
move the discussion to new territory, where he felt at home and
where the issues he understood to be important could be dealt with.
When he went to the legislature, he still did not know a benchmark
from a batch turnaround, but he knew he could defend the expenditure in terms meaningful to him and to the people who would
question him.

Naturally those who can use computing profitably want
more of it; they never have too much. This is true of administrators,
teachers, students, and researchers. But an increase in the computing
budget cannot be justified solely on the grounds that they are now
using all available computing resources and that they want more.

A budget increase must be justified in terms of education rather than of technology. More computing for administrative services must make the college's administration cheaper, more flexible, better adapted to the needs of the people it serves. More computing for student use must make education better than it would be, say, if that money were invested in the library or audio-visual services or faculty salaries. Computing in higher education is not new; it is reasonable to ask for assessment, evaluation, and planning, linking the technical facts with educational realities. However, computing terminology and specialists are at times virtually impossible to understand; yet they are too expensive to ignore. The most frequent and plaintive question one hears from administrators is how this communication gap can be bridged. They ask, How can we evaluate the computing situation on our campus? How can I tell if we are getting our money's worth? Have we got a good director of computing or a bad one? How can we tell if we are doing the right thing? Are my people telling me the truth? The simplest form of the question is, "How much should we be spending for computing?" the assumption apparently being that if you sacrifice the right number of dollars (but not too many), the plague of troublesome questions will not descend.

How is an administrator to manage the computing resources of his institution without himself becoming a technician and without devoting all of his time to what is, after all, only one of a large family of critical resources requiring his attention? The answer is simple, although its implementation may not be easy. He must create an administrative structure that will recognize problems, prevent them if possible, or deal with them as they occur. It should permit technical problems to be solved by technicians, educational problems by educators, and administrative problems by administrators. Only the policy and planning issues critical to the college as a whole should be brought to the attention of the president. But some computing problems are not homogeneous; they must be viewed by different groups of people from different perspectives for a totally satisfactory solution to emerge. As the case study above illustrates, a decision about acquiring a new computer has technical, financial, educational, and managerial components. The organizational structure must be such that problems are routed through the proper channels for solutions to emerge and that no important issue is ever overlooked for long.

In any event, no matter how complex or decentralized some of the services may become, there should be a point in the administrative hierarchy where at least titular control exists, a place where people can go with problems and complaints and a place where innocent users can ask for a road map, to locate a point where they can enter the system and take advantage of the resource. In addition, there should be a structure for planning to analyze needs (as described in Chapter Two), the objectives and style of the particular institution, and the available alternatives (as described in Chapter Three). Policy and planning, monitoring and control are needed in all of the various aspects of computing on campus. The principal aspects of operating a computing facility that require such management are:

*Organization*. Responsibilities for operating the facility must be divided among the users, computing center personnel, and the administration. The users and the financial officers of the college must be assured of proper control over the resource so that it serves the institution and not a small subgroup. These matters demand attention even if the computing is provided from an off-campus source; they are even more critical if the on-campus computing center is providing service to off-campus users.

*Policy*. The expensive and sometimes rare computing resource must be allocated fairly among users vying for preference. The college must be assured that the kind of services being provided are those the users need and that they are being provided in the most efficient manner possible.

*Finance*. How the funds are to be controlled and where they are to come from are naturally important issues. Academic administrators often have a haunting feeling that too much is being spent on computing, while the technical people may have just the opposite reaction to the budget. The financial system should be designed to emphasize and encourage good computer use, which will vary in meaning from campus to campus.

*Instruction*. At all institutions, the question of how students can make the most effective use of computing is an important one, often the most important question.

*Administration.* Administrative use of computing also rep-sents an issue, adding a range of questions about how the computer can be used effectively in the service of the institution as a whole.

*Acquiring systems.* There are many technical issues, largely concerned with acquiring the hardware and software out of which the needed services can be built. Although the nontechnical administrator will not normally be concerned with most of them, they have aspects that are of vital concern.

A few words have already been devoted to some of these issues; the rest of this book deals with each in more detail.

# 6

# ORGANIZATION AND PERSONNEL

When one part of an organization supplies services needed by another, their goals are bound to diverge and their attitudes to differ: even when no money is exchanged, a market-like situation naturally emerges. So it is with campus computing. The director of computing may be seen as a salesman and a supplier, who must see to it that work is attracted to the center up to a comfortable limit. His customers are the academic departments and administrative offices, as represented by the heads of these organizational units. The users (not necessarily the same as the customers) are the individual students, staff, and faculty who send jobs to the computer and receive its output. The final persona in this little drama is the top administration of the institution, whose role it is to see that the other parts get along together and that the economic realities of the institution as a whole are also served.

The difference in point of view among these elements is the

key to understanding the organizational problems of the computing center. The user views computing service as a free and infinitely expandable resource. The focus of his interest is on how computing can be used to further his own objectives: the researcher wants to keep moving ahead with his research; the student wants to hand in his assignments on time; the administrative clerk or analyst wants his report to be on the right desk by Friday morning. They are concerned with their own effectiveness in their jobs and are bound to use whatever resources are available to improve their individual performance. Naturally their concern with the cost/effectiveness of the computing service is low or nonexistent. As shown in Chapter Two, their demands have a strong impact on the cost of computing: they want reliability, stability, convenience, and services that are both broad and deep. But since they do not pay the cost, they have little reason to consider whether they could not accept a slight degradation in service in order to achieve a major economy at the institutional level.

The customer is often the person the user must satisfy and thus is at the root of user demands. The student or junior faculty member wants to get his work done on time in order to satisfy the teacher or the department chairman; the administrative assistant wants the report finished on time because his boss needs it. By representing his organizational unit in the councils of the institution, the customer will also be the one who is asked to speak for the user when service is inadequate. Finally, the customer is in a position to consider cost-effectiveness, since he is aware of the details and purpose of the use and the level and cost of the service. The registrar and not his programmer can tell whether it would be more efficient to do registration some other way; the teacher and not the student can judge whether the educational value of the computing being done is worth the cost in comparison with other alternatives.

The director of computing acts as salesman and also as the supplier of the services he sells. Although he is usually considered the person best able to solve the problems, some peculiar conflicts complicate his role. His first responsibility must be to satisfy the demands of his users; in order to be responsive to them, he must provide the services they ask for and submit the bill to the customers, justifying the cost in terms of user needs. Thus, to avoid user dissatisfaction, he keeps expanding the service and the computing center keeps growing. But in order to pay for this expanding service and justify its existence, he must encourage more and more users to take advantage of the service. Thus he enters a vicious cycle.

This situation encourages expansion of service, more use of computing by more agencies, and higher budgets for computing. It does not seem to provide any controls on cost, any measure of managerial efficiency, or any rewards for a realistic evaluation of the system by any of the participants. One function of good organizational structure and policy is to apply the interests of the people involved to the creation of such incentives and controls.

PURPOSE OF THE ORGANIZATION

As far as possible, an effective computing organization should provide the mechanisms for reaching the following complex and sometimes conflicting objectives:

*Satisfaction of the users' real needs.* Although the needs may be overstated and it may occasionally be necessary to refuse them, it is the user, after all, who must finally be able to get useful work done by the system.

*User recognition of value and scarcity in computing.* The user will consume computing as freely as water unless some incentive for efficiency makes him aware of its value.

*Supplier efficiency.* The supplier, too, should have some incentive for minimizing the cost of computing and discouraging the waste of resources.

*Encouragement of useful growth.* Although efficiency is to be encouraged, the effect should not be to discourage or refuse useful new applications.

*Control of stability and protection of the user.* Many of the technical and political perturbations that occur in the computing center have disastrous and therefore expensive effects on the users. These should be minimized in order to create the orderly and stable system that allows users to work effectively.

*Encouragement of careful and skillful management.* The use of good management techniques should be rewarded and not penalized.

*Evolve goals and policy.* The role of the top administration should not be conflict or crisis resolution but the long-range analysis and control of those aspects of the system that affect the institution as a whole. Top administrators must participate in the development of the long-range computing goals and policy if they are to have confidence that computing is properly serving the institution.

*Provision of a focus for responsibility and authority.* The diffused interests, responsibilities, and authority of computing must be brought together so that enough power exists to make decisions that are responsible and can be carried out. The diffusion of responsibility to the point of stalemate has been the tragedy of computing at more than a few campuses.

### STRUCTURE OF THE ORGANIZATION

If these objectives are to be approached, some form of centralization of computing affairs on the campus seems almost inevitable. At large universities, where major research funds come from off-campus sources, multiple computers seem unavoidable. Even the presence of a central office to coordinate computing may not serve to control the situation completely. In fact, such control may not be desirable. Others claim with equal justice that good reasons support decentralization. Cooperation requires expensive management: a very talented individual with both academic and management skills must serve as the coordinator or director, working full time to hold the pieces together. He needs also the support of a high-level committee to consider plans and policies. Besides all that, in a cooperative setting, everyone from the top administration through the computer staff to the users themselves becomes involved in the politics of priorities and the allocation of scarce resources. In addition to management cost, there is the technical cost of total generality. A center that serves everybody on a moderately large campus must have not only a larger computer (for the economy of scale) but a large library of programs, a flexible system, and a body of consultants who know at least a little bit about everything. The user, even if he wants to do only a very simple piece of work on the computer, must pay for this impressive overhead. Thus, from the point of view of the administration and the user, decentralization (at least to some extent) may be better than arbitrary total centralization.

Because of the management cost of centralization and the technical cost of generality, many medium-to-large institutions with small research budgets accept some degree of decentralization. Separate facilities will be available for academic and administrative use; some mini-computers will be in use in various science departments; some users will occasionally buy remote computing from a commercial or regional center. The real function of the central organization is to foster good computing and not just to create an orderly situation. If apparent confusion and duplication promotes good research and good education, then multiple centers should obviously be encouraged. Yet by and large this is not often the case with multiple centers and competing services. Attempts to create order are generally attempts to improve the quality of computing and the quality of the research and education it serves.

At smaller institutions, of course, centralization may be a necessity. Financial resources may be simply insufficient to permit the dispersion of computing, while individuals or small groups of users may not have the independence to be able to override the interests of the majority. Thus at these institutions the job of coordinating computing is considerably easier, since almost all the users will agree that cooperation is to their own best interests.

But between the centralized computing of the small college and the all-but-unmanageable multiplication of computers in the large university lies the medium-to-large institution, with a teaching rather than a research orientation and with financial problems that encourage economy. Here there is room for difference of opinion and of approach. Some argue that centralization is just as important here as at the small college. In their opinion, the economy of scale in hardware, the advantage in eliminating redundant personnel and service, the potential of load-balancing, and the ability to have a larger machine to operate larger programs all makes centralization imperative. The creation of an organizational structure around computing is not intended just to prevent multiplicity, but to prevent unnecessary and uneconomic multiplicity. Useless duplication results in financial crises that weaken services and debase the overall computing quality. It is thus better to attempt to make computing serve a rational plan from the beginning, so that the interests of the largest number of users and potential users are protected.

COMPUTER CZAR

Coordination and control requires a single administrative officer as the keystone of the computing organization. In a large university he may be a "computer czar" with several computer center directors reporting to him. In a smaller college, he may also be the director of the computing center, with line responsibility for the computer operations and personnel. The role of the computer czar is not technical, athough he must have a good grasp of the technical aspects of the subject. Rather, it is his responsibility both to see the technical side of the questions that are bound to arise and also to understand the role of the computer in the life of the institution. It should be clear to all users, customers, and suppliers of service that the czar is an academic officer and not a technician.

Two forms of czar seem to be emerging on today's campuses. At a few institutions, all university-wide information services (including computing, television, audio-visual services, and even the library) are the responsibility of one individual at the vice-presidential level. More common is the "assistant to the provost for computing" or the "director of information services" who reports to the chief academic officer of the institution, the provost or academic vice-president. If he is not to be too closely identified with one user group or another, he must be placed fairly high in the organization. His role may include line responsibility for computing decisions or he may be considered to occupy a staff position. In job descriptions, one reads "He will assist the provost." or "He will advise the president." His primary responsibility is to assure that decisions are technically viable, managerially sound, and in the interest of the institution's academic goals. He should also attempt to make the long-range development of computing on campus conform to the objectives listed at the beginning of this chapter.

As a force for control, the czar conflicts with the traditions of academic freedom which would allow members of the academic community to do as they please in acquiring services from agents of their own choice. In exercising his authority he is bound to be unpopular with many of his colleagues. For this reason it is important that he himself have an academic background and be seen as an academician rather than as primarily a technician or an administrator. Many observers feel that like other members of the administration, he should be changed periodically: after a few years, he should go back to being a computer user, and allow some other individual to become the czar. On the other hand, despite his title, the czar does not really exercise much in the way of control or authority. He has friendly persuasion ("But haven't you considered the attractive possibilities of doing it my way?"), the ear of the provost, and the threat of a veto of financial expenditures. But even this financial control may not mean much, for neither he nor the provost has much control over "dean's funds" or special grants from government agencies.

The position of the czar is often supported by a committee, which may be called the "computer executive committee" or "computer advisory committee" or "computer policy committee." This committee also may report to the provost or president and be responsible for advising him on computer-related matters. The committee usually consists of representatives of the departments that are the major customers for computing, plus the chief financial officer of the institution, and the computing director or directors. This group represents the concentration of a larger mass of influence and power than the czar, and possibly even the provost, can muster. If this group reaches consensus and supports a recommendation made by the czar, a decision can be made and enforced. This structure thus allows important issues to be reviewed and considered by a large share of the political power on the campus.

### DIRECTOR OF COMPUTING

In contrast with the czar, the director of computing is a technician and a manager. He will be current on the technicalities of computing and also represent some skill and experience in management. In the early days of computing in higher education, the director was likely primarily an academic—probably a professor of mathematics who dabbled in computers. As the technical problems became more specialized and the demands on the director's time greater, he usually retired and left the center to the control of his second in command, who was a computer technician or a programmer by training. As the center grows and this technician finds himself out of his depth, he is being replaced at a number of representative campuses by a man with considerable managerial skills in addition to a technical background. At any event, if the college has a czar to represent the educational or institutional component, the computing director must be selected for his technical and managerial capabilities. If he is both czar and director, then he must have all three talents and must be selected with even greater care.

Obviously, the director should report to the czar, although this may sometimes be difficult to arrange. If special-purpose centers exist on the campus, their directors may naturally report to the chief officers of the departments they serve. If, for instance, there is a medical school computing center, it will naturally owe allegiance to the medical school as well as the computing establishment on campus.

Many campus computer center directors report to the chief business officers of their colleges, particularly when their centers serve both administrative and academic users. Although the chief business officers and the computing directors who report to them may deny it, it is usually obvious to a visitor that in these cases the academic personnel have small voice in managing the computer and make small use of it. It seems reasonable to predict that as such centers come to serve the academic community better, the responsibility for their management must be passed from the business officer to a more general officer of the college, such as the provost or the president.

The director of computing will meet regularly with a user committee composed of representatives from major groups of users. This is by no means the same as the czar's committee, which assesses plans and determines policy. The members of the user committee meet with the director in order to express their problems to those providing the services and to attempt to make the center management understand their difficulties and their needs. It also serves for communication in the other direction: the computing director can inform the users of his problems and difficulties and try to make them understand why it is not always possible to comply with their demands. He may also use the committee to assess user reactions to potential changes in kinds or levels of service. Because of their focus on service rather than cost, on effectiveness rather than efficiency, user committees make a bad organ for planning; that function is better performed by the more broadly-based policy committee.

COMPUTING CENTER STAFF

On the staff of a small center, a single person may perform several functions. The czar/director, for example, may also be the systems programmer and will manage the center's business affairs; his secretary will be responsible for the library and user communications. Despite the size of a center, all the functions of a large center are present, even if divided between only two people. I shall therefore explore the organization of a typical large center.

Figure 1 shows the organization of computing at Hypothetical University. The director has six groups reporting to him. Responsible for running the machines is the operations group, which includes keypunch operators as well as computer operators and part-time student help as well as full-time professionals. The systems maintenance group keeps the software working, making the alterations and corrections necessary to systems created elsewhere, and developing special systems when necessary.

The applications staff is a group of programmers and analysts available to work on user projects. Some academic centers and many administratively-oriented data processing centers have such a staff. In administrative processing, it is inefficient for each office to have its own analysts and programmers, just as it is inefficient for them to have their own computers, so a staff created to serve them all is attached to the computing center. For academic programming, however, the user generally wants to do the programming himself, of if not, then have it done by someone who has at least a rudimentary knowledge of the researcher's field.

The business office of the computing center is responsible for keeping track of resource usage, accounting, billing, and the allocation of resources even when money is not involved.

The information functions lumped under the name "library" are several. First, the center maintains a collection of documents

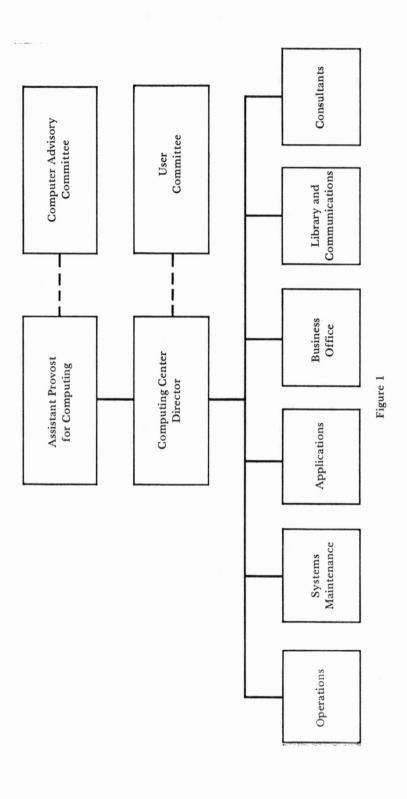

Figure 1

that may be of interest to the users. Second, the center may issue a periodical newsletter to inform users of changes or additions to the system, special problems other users have experienced, and changes in rates, priorities, or times of availability. Finally, the center may offer brief, noncredit courses in programming in various languages. These are popular at many campuses, both among faculty and students.

The last group is composed of consultants for user problems. A user may get back from the system some response that he does not understand, for example, his program in FORTRAN could not be compiled for reason 714.3W. But when he looks in his manual, he finds no explanation of 714.3W. Another user has written a program to evaluate a function and, although he has done everything correctly, the results are wrong by such a wide margin that some error must have been made. Another user would like some advice on available languages for list-processing applications. All of these users call upon the center's consultant staff. A large center may have a staff of people whose primary responsibility is to act as user consultants. At others, this may be a part-time job for programmers. At most institutions, this service is actually provided by student assistants, who are the first line of contact for users. When they cannot solve a problem unassisted, they will call on the full-time professionals of the programming staff. When users are located remotely and served by telephone lines, the consultants will probably also be available in this way, in which case the user should be able to call the consultant, explain his problem, and get help without visiting the center.

It is worth noting that if some or all of the campus' computing is done remotely, most of the reasons for having most of these functions available on the campus still exist. The functions of the czar, the director, and the two committees are essentially unchanged. Planning and policy-making must still go on. If the computer is located elsewhere, the operations and systems maintenance staffs can surely be reduced, but some minimum amount of hardware will probably continue to exist on the campus and continue to demand operation and maintenance. Also, the business office, the library, and the consultant services are still needed, no matter where the computer is located.

Even if the remote center, for example, the regional computation center at the state university one hundred miles away, provides these services, they will probably not be in the form most helpful to the users. Essentially, the regional center is selling its services wholesale to the college computing center, and this center then retails services to individual users. This is true of all the services, information and consulting as well as access to hardware and software. The local center, for instance, will provide consultation services and a library for users on the local campus. When users ask for documents that the library does not have or ask the consultant for advice he cannot provide, the local center staff may then turn to the remote center for assistance.

Suppose there are multiple centers on the campus—how much of this organization must be duplicated? The answer depends on the nature of the different centers and the kind of overlap that exists in their services. Wherever one finds hardware, he also finds operators, systems maintenance, accounting, and consultation. If some of these functions are coordinated in order to circumvent the obvious inefficiency of duplicating the entire structure, then in fact some centralization is taking place, for whoever controls the systems programmers, the applications staff, and the information functions is beginning to control the hardware as well. Even if several unconnected pieces of hardware are located on the campus, the organization is coordinated and unified.

### SUPERCENTERS AND ORGANIZATION

This situation is altered, however, when off-campus computer use dominates the campus scene. If the college decides to acquire its computing from an off-campus agency, it must see itself as a customer acquiring a service useful to the administrative, research, and instructional activities of the college. The college must be concerned about the cost-effectiveness of what it is buying; it must use (or sometimes create) avenues to inform the supplier of problems with hardware, software, or policies; it must evaluate alternatives so that the supplier is never seen out of the context of other possible ways of getting the needed services. It must be adamant in making sure that it is receiving the maximum benefit for the financial resources expended. At the same time, of course, the central agency that acquires the service may be retailing it to the users. In this case, all of the functions of the computing center described above will have to be performed.

The question of off-campus computer use is quite different if the college or university itself begins serving off-campus users. In this case the college must realize that it is acquiring a customer different in kind from the on-campus user who is part of the same organizational unit as the computing center. The center has two alternatives: it can dispose of excess capacity by selling it for whatever it can get, or it can adapt itself to providing a service for which a market exists. In the first case, a university may have spare resources, which can be made available to any institution that wants to buy them. If no users turn up, nothing is really lost. If some do and they are content to take what they can get, their financial contribution can be looked upon more or less as a windfall. If the users do not like the service once they try it, they are free to go away. In this case, users who have no unusual requirements are probably served well enough. Those who make demands are ignored. Little needs to be said about the management in this case, because it is managed exactly as if no off-campus users were present and no accommodation is made for the sake of this shift in the market.

In the second case, the university decides for one reason or another to make computing available to other institutions, aware that the kind of computing they require may not be identical to that required by the on-campus users. A shift in management posture is required to serve these users. The center must perform all of the functions already described, but in a broadened context. The advisory committee, for instance, should include representation by off-campus customers. If these customer colleges are really supporting the center materially and the center is trying to meet their needs, they should have some voice in the establishment of policy and long-range plans.

The library and consulting functions of the university computing center must also be broadened if it is to serve the off-campus user, for these functions are quite possibly of greater interest and value to these users than the computer itself. The smaller college, which is the primary potential customer for this kind of service, will be less sophisticated than the on-campus user and will be in special need of consultants and library service. In North Carolina, the smaller colleges deal with the TUCC only indirectly, through a state agency which provides consultants on educational methodology and curriculum, as well as "circuit rider" consultants who go out to the colleges periodically and discuss user problems. Such services are of critical importance to the smaller college, the remote college, or the college that has not had a significant prior exposure to computing. The off-campus users may thus require more specialized service than the computing center is accustomed to provide for its on-campus users. Some administrators may even find that they require too much service, considering the amount of computing they buy. But if the idea of regional computing or super-centralization is to be successful, this kind of service will be the critical factor.

Assuming that a university is aware of the cost, why should it want to serve off-campus users? First, the financial crunch and the adoption of a businesslike attitude at the university may make it appear desirable, even at the cost of expanded service. Second, the university itself may represent too small a user base to support an optimum level of service. Off-campus users help broaden this base, even if they must be developed into sophisticated users over a long period of time. Third, the university may consider itself responsible for supporting its neighboring colleges in the development of new resources and techniques. Finally, the university may be coerced by a state agency into serving the computing needs of some off-campus users.

And why should the small college be willing to take the risks of acquiring its computing in this way? First, financial realities may make it necessary for the college to consider this alternative as a reasonable approach to acquiring maximum service for minimum cost. Second, an analysis of alternatives may reveal that this is an opportunity to get computing that has the proper characteristics, is dependable, and has the necessary controls—a combination that is hard to beat. Third, the college can obtain information and technical assistance from this arrangement that would not be available otherwise. They will also be able to take advantage of the experience and knowledge of the university, while hopefully avoiding its mistakes. Fourth, like the university, they may be coerced.

If such an arrangement succeeds, the user group will have expanded to the point where the university depends on them and they on it and both will take care to see that the relationship remains technically and administratively healthy and financially viable. This attitude of care produces some evident consequences. At one center, set up to provide computing on a regional basis, the advisory committee was initially made up of college presidents and vice-presidents. As time went on, other concerns drew away the top administrators, who were replaced by technical personnel from their staffs. But when the users began to depend on the system for vital services, its continuance became critical. Then the level of the committee members began to rise, eventually reaching the vice-presidential, if not the presidential, level once again.

RESOURCES AND REFERENCES

The analogy between academic computing and a marketplace with users, customers, and suppliers was first pointed out by Einar Stefferud and appeared in a *Datamation* article (Mosmann and Stefferud, 1971). The same magazine contained a pair of articles on the pros and cons of resource sharing between academic and administrative users (Ralston, 1971, and Roberts, 1971).

Many books have been published on the general question of the organization and management of commercial data processing installations. Some of these will naturally be applicable to the academic computer. One of the best (and briefest) is Withington (1972); Ditri, Shaw, and Atkins (1971) is also recommended.

A series of articles of great interest will be found in the reports of two conferences for computing center directors, sponsored by the University of Colorado: *Seminar for the Directors of Academic Computing Centers, Final Report* (1970) and *Second Annual Seminar for Directors of Academic Computing Centers, Proceedings* (1971).

It is the intention of the computing center at the University of Colorado to continue holding these seminars and to publish proceedings that include the papers prepared for and delivered at the seminars. Thus further documents can be expected. The meetings themselves also represent a resource. Information about them can be obtained from the computing center at the University of Colorado. The meetings and newsletter of the Special Interest Group on University Computer Centers have already been mentioned; it should certainly be regarded as a primary resource in matters of computer center organization and management. The Special Interest Group on Computer Systems Installation Management (sigcosim) is another activity of the Association for Computing Machinery and its meetings and publications will also be of interest in this context.

# 7

# SETTING POLICY

Many of the questions that plague the campus computing system hinge on philosophical issues regarding the purpose of the center and its role within the larger structure of the college as a whole. When no effort is made to bring these basic issues to the light and to answer some of the fundamental questions, current crises must be dealt with on the basis of expediency and no permanent or orderly solution is possible. Thus, if the life of computing on the campus is to be calm and productive, these basic issues must be dealt with, by discussing and deciding on the purpose and role of the computing system, and then establishing an enlightened computing policy consistent with this philosophy and the goals of the college. Of the numerous problems that arise because these issues are not resolved, three are particularly in evidence at many computing centers of all sizes and types.

First, technical issues are confused with political issues. As a result, both hardware and software systems are designed to satisfy political pressures rather than a real need. A few vocal and powerful individuals dictate system design, with the result that the system handles a few large and complex programs well, but at the expense of the majority of users, who have small and simple problems.

Second, consequence of the lack of policy is a timidity that prevents the consideration of radical alternatives. Despite the wide range of options available, as described in Chapter Three, many institutions, particularly smaller ones, cling to the small on-campus center for no reason other than their unwillingness to consider changes. Alternatives of inter-institutional cooperation and consequent risk-sharing by small colleges are largely unexplored; so are the more complex structures for larger institutions. Some writers have suggested that the special characteristics of academic computing (time of day and time of year usage, for instance) would make it economical to consider joint projects with industry so as to balance the load. This alternative too has by and large been left unconsidered. All of these alternatives merit more consideration and attention than they have received. But without policy, it is too difficult to evaluate them and the chance of making a very bad mistake is high.

Third, an institution without a basic policy is usually unwilling or unable to commit itself to long-range plans. Without a clear understanding of what the goals of computing are, the institution cannot commit itself to either a particular direction or particular mileposts to be achieved over the next few years. This inability to plan results in higher costs (because direction changes frequently) and poor service (because users cannot rely on continuity and stability).

Agreement on the merit of philosophy, goals, and policy may be general; but agreement on how to create such a statement and what it should consist of is not so widespread. Yet some guidance can be given to those who are ready to try. First of all, it is important to realize that a commitment of this kind cannot be made by any one individual on the campus. It needs the broad support that the computer advisory committee described in Chapter Six can provide. This committee should be responsible for drafting and publishing a document that makes it clear what computing means on their campus, how issues will be settled, and how the center will be made to work so as to serve the goals set for it.

The basic document will naturally be fairly general. Perhaps the best way to sketch out its possible content is to list the kinds of questions it should address: (1) What is the function of the computing establishment, in terms of the ideals or goals of the college as a whole? (2) Whom does it serve? In cases of conflict, whom does it serve first? (3) Who determines the policy of the establishment? In cases of differences of opinion, who has the last word: the administration, the computing center management, the users, or some other body? (4) What level of service and what style of operation will best satisfy the objectives? Should the center be run in a formal or informal fashion? Will the user receive lots of guidance or will he be expected to learn by making his own mistakes? (5) How will planning be done? What is the relationship of the computing plan to the long-range institutional plan, if one exists? (6) How important is good computing to the college? What is it worth in terms of money and in terms of the attention and time of the busiest and most talented members of both the faculty and the administration? (7) Who will decide how much money is going to be spent on computing: the users, the computing director, the chief budget officer of the college? (8) Is the computing center a business run by the college for its own convenience or is it an unofficial, not-for-credit academic department, where research and education are carried out?

Few institutions have in fact produced statements that make all these matters clear. Yet a visitor to a campus where computing is well managed can discover quickly that answers to these questions exist and are well understood by all concerned. Even here, however, one is tempted to encourage the faculty and staff to write down what they know; unwritten laws are subject to strange and secret amendment.

At institutions where these questions cannot be answered, a policy vacuum exists. Policy will be established to suit the loudest voice and the center may be run to meet the needs of the most powerful group of users—possibly a few research projects. This may or may not be the most valuable service that could be provided, but how is one to know, when no one has bothered to ask what "valuable" means in this context?

In addition to providing some insight into how these general questions are to be answered, a policy statement should deal with some more specific matters. This statement will provide the computing personnel the guidance they need to manage their day-to-day relations with their users; it will also provide the assurances the users need so that they can make use of the center with confidence and plan the integration of computing into the instruction, research, and administrative affairs of the college.

The statement should enumerate the services the center expects to offer, described in terms of the dimensions listed in Chapter Two. In particular, the statement should deal specifically with hardware and software availability, depth of consulting capability to be maintained, system and programming support personnel available to the users, and other services, such as library, non-credit courses, or keypunching.

The statement should also decide what user community is to be served by the center: students and faculty? Administrative personnel? Other campuses? It should also decide whether all the users are to be treated alike, or whether there are different classes to be served differently.

The mode of operation, including any and all restrictions on user access should be discussed: What must a person do in order to become a user? How close can he get to the actual machinery?

The qualifications, responsibilities, and authority of the czar (if there is to be one), the manager, and (at least in a moderate-to-large center) the assistant manager should be spelled out. The general characteristics and responsibilities needed to provide the required services may also be treated.

Perhaps the most important paragraphs in a statement of policy are those devoted to resource allocation, provided they are clear and can actually be implemented. If access to the service is to be limited in some way, the mechanism for allocating the resources to the users must be spelled out. If the available computing, consulting, and programming services are to be divided up among the using departments, offices, and projects on a sane basis, the rules for this allocation must be made clear.

Resource allocation is often taken to mean only dividing up the time on the computer. Although this is certainly important, it is not the only aspect of the subject. Since only a finite number of software systems can be acquired and maintained, the policy should make it clear how the center staff decides whether additions should be made to this library. In other words, when are the desires of some segment of the user community great enough to warrant expending general funds to satisfy their special need?

Priority is another aspect of resource allocation, but because of its importance it needs independent consideration. When congestion occurs at peak load, the computing center staff needs guidance in resolving conflicts. Whenever two people want access to the same resource at the same time, a rule of priority must be invoked.

If a charge against some account is to be made for services rendered, the charging policy should be spelled out in general terms. It is also necessary to explain why the policy exists and the objective that it is to accomplish. This assists the computing personnel in setting the specific rates for their services. (Chapter Eight deals in more detail with questions of finance.)

Accountability may be designed into the system by such mechanisms as advisory committees and user committees, which ensure that those who depend on the services of the computing center can influence its operation when the service appears inadequate or unresponsive. If the administrative staff, the faculty, and the students are to be held responsible for getting their work done on time and if this work depends on computing resources, then the supplier of this resource must be made accountable to them in some way—the users must have some influence over the center when their ability to meet their commitments is in jeopardy.

The way in which the computing budget is to be made up should be detailed. The role of the users, the customers, and the computing staff should be described, since each has an interest in the budget and wants to know how he can exert his influence on it.

The policy of the college with regard to computer centralization should be made explicit, so that the staff and the committees will know if they are to take permissive or restrictive attitudes regarding the proliferation of multiple special-purpose computers and the use of off-campus facilities not under the control of the central computing establishment. In particular, since this is a general philosophical statement, the rules should be set down that govern the decision as to whether a user is permitted to acquire his own computer or to use some alien facility.

The responsibilities of the various groups interested in computing for producing or approving long-range computing plans should be delineated. In particular, the role of the user must be made clear, particularly his ability to enforce his requirement for stability of service.

The relation between the center and other parts of the college will have been covered in other sections of the policy statement; if more needs to be added, it can appear here. It may also be necessary to describe the relationship between the college computing center and other interested or influential agencies, such as a community guidance group, or a statewide regulatory or advisory body.

A policy statement that covers all of these matters (or as many as appear relevant to a particular institution) provides the guidance necessary for the smooth, orderly, and useful operation of a computing service. Its clarity and specific guidance mean that problems can be resolved at an appropriate level without the further involvement of the advisory committee or the intervention of the college president to resolve heated disagreement.

No document that covers so many aspects of the subject—particularly if it is clear and detailed enough to guide the center's management—can be expected to stand unmodified for very long. People often agree to any policy at all, until they learn how it impinges on their freedom; then they want the entire subject reopened and reconsidered. Changes in available resources, along with growth and shifts in user needs, will demand that policy be altered or expanded. Upon the advisory committee rests the continuing responsibility to consider prospective policy changes.

Given a policy statement, it is the responsibility of the staff to attempt as economically as possible to acquire resources, convert them into user services, and to allocate them among the users, all within the boundaries established.

### SUPERCENTERS AND NETWORKS

In the preceding discussion of the management of computing, I assumed that the computing establishment on the campus serves one campus only or that at least part of a college's service is provided from an on-campus source. The advent of the super-center, the computer center that serves more than a single campus, complicates but does not significantly change the need for goals, philosophy, and policy. As for the campus that uses the service of a super-center, it still must have a policy for its on-campus establishment; even if its hardware is limited to a terminal. It also must assume the role of a customer (see Chapter Six) in its dealings with the super-center, becoming an influence on the management structure there and participating in the development of policy at a higher level.

The institution that houses an on-campus center that is also used as a regional resource by other institutions has a difficult management problem. The regional center has a broad and diversified user community, but usually lacks the cohesive influence of a central administration. Yet the problems the super-center faces are much the same as those of an ordinary center and demand similar solutions; thus a policy statement is called for. Its most critical function is to clarify the responsibility of the super-center to external users and to its own parent institution. Are external users to be treated as second-class users? If not, what is the center's real relationship with its parent college and why should it be housed there at all? And, if it is really only offering second-class service, honesty requires that the potential customer know this, too.

The problems of a distributed network in which the member colleges both accept jobs from off-campus users and submit jobs to other centers is something else again. Some writers have begun to draw attention to the problems of network management. If the nodes on such a network are college and university campuses, then it seems clear that such a system is inherently unmanageable, for no agency is in a position to coerce such a group into conformity with a plan, even if the plan is in their own best interests. On the other hand, a college joining a network is taking on both technical and managerial problems. Such a college should have its own house in order—have a clear understanding of its own policy and goals— before it accepts new problems. On this basis, then, the computing service advisory committee at the college can judge how external customers will affect the college computing establishment, and how the availability of external services will jeopardize it, the two key issues in joining a network.

### PRIORITIES

The earlier discussion of the need for policy cited the use of priorities as one means of allocating scarce resources. Priority is a a much-abused subject, because it connotes preferential treatment.

But having priorities only means having a rule for making a decision when alternative actions are possible: when, to choose the simplest case, the computer operator finds two decks of cards on the "input" shelf, which one should he pick up first? An allocation system is no substitute for a priority rule in answering this question, unless the computing resource is allocated to such a fine level of detail that no job gets put on the shelf until the previous one stops running. What the operator needs is a simple rule. In most cases, the simplest rule is the one first adopted: "First come, first served." The decks are put on the shelf at the bottom of a stack and the operator is to take them off at the top of the stack. This is a perfectly acceptable rule of priority.

When conflicts arise and work slows down, a more complicated scheme may emerge. This usually means having more than one stack on the shelf. At some institutions, there are two stacks: one for administrative and one for academic work. One stack is always emptied before the other one is begun. It is possible that different priorities may be given to the two stacks at different times of the day: academic work is always done first from noon to six p.m.; administrative work is given first priority in the morning and at night.

A third alternative is to separate the jobs into different stacks depending on the characteristics of the jobs, rather than on who submits them. All jobs that take less than one minute and require no special set-up (mounting tapes, disk packs, special paper on the printer, etc.) will be in one stack and all jobs that take longer in another; the short jobs will always be run before the long jobs. A further distinction may be made between long jobs and very long jobs. Perhaps a category will be needed for very, very long jobs.

When the priority scheme gets more complicated than this, the analogy of several stacks is imperfect because there may be as many stacks as there are jobs. At some large installations, a unique priority is defined for each job whenever a decision has to be reached about what to do next. Each job is evaluated in terms of its estimated running time, the amount of memory it requires, the length of time the job has already been waiting (for extra long jobs may never get run at all unless this is considered), and even the amount of service the submitting user has already had that day.

In addition to all these considerations, the user may be

asked to make his own statement of priority; this soon becomes inflated to the point that all jobs are labelled URGENT. Some reward must be given to users for selecting a low priority. Usually, it is financial: the rates for low priority are less than the rates for high priority: an urgent priority label may triple the normal cost of running a job, while a low priority label may discount it by 25 to 50 percent. This reward system works very well from the point of view of the computing center, shifting the load from the peak hours to evenings and weekends. However, it asks the user to trade the amount of computing available to him (for this is all that his money usually means) for greater responsiveness. This is not a meaningful trade-off for most users. Further, it does not always work, even for the computing center. Toward the end of the fiscal year, many users who have been budgeting their allocation frugally find that they have a surplus. They then convert their surplus into responsiveness by increasing the priority of all their work. Enough users like this can destroy the whole mechanism, because the resources do not in fact exist to supply the demand that is created.

Each of these schemes has its disadvantages, but one of them, or some novel technique not yet invented, must be employed if the computer operator with two decks on the input shelf (or his automated counterpart in the monitor system of a large computer) is to reach a decision.

### RESOURCES AND REFERENCES

On the subject of policy statements for academic computing centers, I can offer little documentation. Ditri, Shaw, and Atkins (1971) is a useful survey of the functions of management in data processing. Valuable ideas and inputs to policy discussions are found in Lykos (1971) and Gillespie (1970).

Some interesting reports and suggestions have been published on the subjects of allocation and priority. A terse and clear enunciation of the problem of allocation is found in a letter to the editor of *Science* (Simon, 1966). Nielsen (1970) and Gillespie (1971) offer insights into some aspects of the question. Sutherland (1968) describes an interesting and totally unusual system of allocation in which users bid for computer time by auction. The specific technique is probably not widely applicable but the willingness to try a completely new approach to this old problem certainly is. Stefferud (1968) discusses the importance of economics in the solution of scheduling problems.

# 8

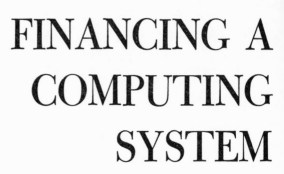

# FINANCING A COMPUTING SYSTEM

In computerland, one matter is always critical: money. Technical, managerial, and educational issues all cast dollar-shaped shadows, for decisions in those areas must ultimately be translated into computer dollars and the bill paid. Yet few decisions in computing are made on a purely economic basis. The important question is always what is being bought (education, research, community service) rather than what it costs. Money is not the only reality, but it is an interesting transformation of reality into a one-dimensional column of figures.

### TYPICAL BUDGET PATTERN

At most institutions, computing appears as a single line item in the budget. This makes it easy to see how much computing costs, but it does not tell us much about where the money goes or what it is used for. Nevertheless, the budget process at a typical university is worth exploring. At Hypothetical University, the process begins when department heads, including the computing center director, prepare budget requests for the following year. The computing director may simply look at his records, extrapolate trends, add and subtract amounts here and there because of particular projects, and sum up the anticipated center use. He then translates this information into additional hardware, software, and personnel: reduces these to a dollar figure; and submits this to the budget office. If he is particularly cautious or feels in need of support for his budget requests, he sends a questionnaire to the other departments, asking how much they anticipate using the center during the next year. He then uses these numbers rather than his own extrapolations. They are not necessarily better, but they do distribute the responsibility for the bad guesses a little more widely.

After the customary discussions and possible reductions, the budget is finalized. The director, knowing what he can actually spend, can now make concrete plans, translating the budget figure into people, software, and machinery. But he must also be concerned about the allocation of the resulting service, for if computing is already paid for out of this lump item in the budget, the service is essentially free to all comers. Who is going to get it? At Hypothetical U., this decision is the responsibility of the Computer Advisory Committee, which receives from the computing director a description of how the computing resources were used during the past year and how he anticipates demand will change the next year. On this basis the committee allocates the available computing services to the schools and departments that will be the customers.

But computing service is a complex affair. How can this multi-dimensional matrix, this $n$-space pie, be sliced up? Easily, reduce the dimensions back to the single one of money and allocate it as though it were dollars. If, let us say, H. U.'s computing budget is one million dollars, then it is assumed that the services made available by the center are worth one million dollars to its users. The allocations to the schools and departments are in dollars and should total one million. Of course, no one really gives these departments one million dollars: what they are given is credit for so many dollars'

worth of service from the campus computing center: they are
dollars that can only be spent for one thing from one source. The
term "funny money" is frequently used to describe these kinds of
funds.

The advisory committee, then, allocates one million dollars'
worth of computing among the using departments, first priority
usually going to research projects bringing in real dollars. The rest
is allocated according to need. The decision is made largely on historic precedent and the predictions of the director. Some of the
departments may complain that their needs have been slighted,
thereby winning a change in the allocation. However, the recommendations of the director usually carry the day since he is, after
all, the one who has the data.

After the departments and schools receive their allocations,
they go through another cycle, suballocating the funny money to
different research projects and particular courses of instruction.
Each user tries to keep close to his budget after it has thus been set
down. If he runs out, he must appeal to the advisory committee for
a further allocation, which he may not get. If, on the other hand, he
is too frugal and ends the year having used less than he was allocated, he will probably get a smaller allocation the following year.

Thus the situation seems admirably controlled: available
computing, allocated computing, and used computing are all in
perfect balance. In fact, however, this equilibrium may be somewhat illusory. The advisory committee, it turns out, only allocates
95 percent of the available computing to the schools, reserving a
little for emergencies; the deans of the schools, too, hold back a
little when they suballocate to the departments. And the department
chairmen set aside some funds when passing out computing for research and instruction. The professor, in his turn, does not allocate
quite all of the computing to his students since he does not trust them
any more than those up the pipeline trusted him to budget effectively.
And the students, finally, not knowing how much of their allocation
they will need for assignments not yet seen are likely to be excessively
frugal at the beginning of the term and then wasteful toward the
end. In general, everyone in the system helps to create an artificial
scarcity at the beginning of the year and then a real scarcity at the

end of the year, when everyone attempts to use up his left-over allocations before they are lost.

Although very popular, budgeting by allocation is not the only kind possible. Many institutions, including some large state and private universities, prefer a form of budgeting in which the customers make more of the decisions and the computing center director and the advisory committee play a more passive role. In this plan, the computing center has no budget of its own; computing appears in the university budget as part of the budget for the various departments and research projects that are the customers of the computing center. The growing popularity of program budgets seems to encourage this kind of planning, although it too has disadvantages.

### ALTERNATIVE SCHEMES

The computing director at Exemplary College does not have any role in the budget cycle or in planning for the college as a whole, although some of his customers may ask his advice as they make their estimates for the following year. When the budget is complete and each department has specified how they expect to spend their financial resources, the director can go through the budget, sum up all the allocations for computing, and then know the total of his budget. His job is then to produce the maximum service he can, knowing the total amount he can expect to receive. His problem is rather more difficult than that of his colleague at Hypothetical University. He finds himself, in fact, in a situation that is almost impossible: he is expected to maintain a balance between a highly variable income (over which he has little control) and a relatively fixed cost resource (over which he can exert little short-range control). Since he cannot alter his hardware configuration or manning levels overnight, he may find himself with a deficit or a profit before the end of the year.

On the other hand, argue administrators at Exemplary College, although the computing center has more headaches, the situation for the college as a whole is much healthier. The customers can decide whether they want to ask for money for computing or some other form of service. It is they, and not the computing director, who decide how much computing is good for them to have and to use. If there is doubt as to whether the college may be spending too much for computing, it is not the computing director who must defend this expenditure but the customers, who can argue from value obtained. (Then again, it is likely that no one will question the amount being spent for computing if it is invisible in the budget, if the funds appear where they are used, in the service of the various departments and offices.)

Many people argue that neither of these models is adequate and that a totally different approach should be taken in providing computing services for higher education. The computing center should appear as a line item in the budget but should not be allocated to users, even in the form of funny money. Computing should appear to the ultimate user as a totally free resource like the library, an analogy always used in this context. Anyone with a legitimate use for service should be able to go to the center and get it. Presumably, some controls must be placed on what a legitimate purpose is. But, if it is legitimate, it must be acknowledged. The job of the computing center is to maintain resources adequate to respond to all foreseeable users. Since use is dictated by need rather than artificial financial constraints, it should not be subject to the erratic fluctuations experienced at Hypothetical and Exemplary Colleges.

This approach has been used with considerable success by small colleges and by larger ones when they were making their first, tentative explorations of computer use. When all the users are really experimenting to find out what computing can do, it is difficult to allocate resources and unrealistic to expect them to be able to justify the cost of what they are doing. When the total investment is not large, the financial controls necessary to support a budgeting system for computing may not be worth the trouble. Finally, there may be enough of the resource available, so that it is not necessary to place constraints upon its use.

However, when the user community grows in size and the budget for computing skyrockets, this approach usually has to be abandoned. If neither the user nor the customer has any concept of what his work is costing, use is encouraged without consideration of effectiveness. It is also impossible for any agency in this situation to evaluate alternative expenditures. The real difficulty, however, that destroys the feasibility of this method is the difference between funded research (which presumably should pay its fair share of the cost of computing used) and university sponsored use. It is not possible to treat computing like a library for some users and like a bookstore for others.

ACHIEVING BALANCE

None of these three basic budgeting schemes seems ideal; in fact, each has what appears to be a fatal flaw. If computing is a free resource, users have no way to correlate cost with value and total college computing costs are bound to expand beyond reasonable limits. If the computer committee and the facility director are responsible for planning and allocation, the supplier is given control of the resource and has little incentive for economy, careful management, or user responsiveness. It is also very difficult to make any reasonable judgment at this level as to what the college as a whole "ought" to be spending for computing. But if control is given to the user, where it would seem reasonably to belong, the director of computing is given the impossible task of planning a steady resource to meet a fluctuating demand. In a good budgeting system, a balance must be achieved between control by the user (which insures quality and economy of service) and control by the supplier (which assures a balanced budget and stability). Although refinements can be made to each of the three schemes described, no fourth alternative has yet been invented that achieves this balance easily.

Consider the case of one midwestern state university. The computing center has in the past made several radical shifts in direction, with the acquisition of incompatible hardware. As a result, users have come to distrust the stability of the center and much computing is now done by other means. But stability has now been achieved and the center management is attempting to attract users back to the center. At the same time, however, the current system is operating at a deficit. If the center is to cut its costs, another major shift in hardware is necessary, alienating more users; but if it is to keep its promise of stability, new sources of revenue or subsidy must be found.

If the on-campus computing center director has a difficult job, the manager of a network is not much better off. Because the on-campus director is so beset by problems of maintaining a balance between his fixed-cost operation and his variable income, he views any kind of off-campus service as a further danger, regardless of its potential value. Bertrand Herzog, director of the Michigan MERIT system, points out that the fear of losing money is the great inhibitor of networks. A distributed network needs money to start the flow of work back and forth. But each of the facilities on the network may be unwilling to allow any money to flow out until some flows in since they are obligated to operate in the black. But if each of the nodes of the network is managed in this way, we are left with a network of sellers of service and no buyers at all.

Some efforts toward resolving these paradoxes have been moderately successful; not all computing directors operate on the edge of hysteria. One major factor in stabilizing the demand upon the on-campus center is the combining of academic and administrative use into a single facility. The administrative load is predictable and lends the combined facility some of the characteristics academic users want. Another alternative is that selected by Harvard: in addition to attempting to smooth out fluctuations in use, it reduced long-term commitments to a fixed-cost resource by minimizing on-campus hardware.

A further suggestion made is that, in order to achieve a balance between user control and supplier control, users be given some funny money (which the on-campus facility is sure to get) and some real money (which the user can spend off campus or at the campus facility).

#### FINANCE AS A VEHICLE OF CONTROL

Proponents of the library analogy argue that the user should not have to be concerned with the cost of the services he uses. But the analogy is inadequate, for the incremental cost of one user borrowing one book from a library is beneath the level of notice, while the same is not true of the user of computing. If the growth of computer use is to be restrained to what is important and necessary for educational purposes, the user needs to have some reminders of the value and the scarcity of the resources put at his disposal. Further, once he is aware of this, money, even funny money, can be used as a vehicle of traffic control, of managing the market so as to create better and more economical computing. Computing has, for instance, different values at different times: more jobs are submitted at two in the afternoon than at two in the morning, on Wednesday than on Sunday, during the semester than between semesters. The computing center staff must balance this load since it is not reasonable to build a system to handle peak load only to be idle at every other time. Users who help the computer center staff achieve this objective should be rewarded, one way being to give them a discount on their computing. They may also be given a discount for long-term contracts since these would aid the computer center staff in its long-range planning. The pricing scheme, however, needs constant adjustment and tuning to create and maintain a workable system. Care must be taken that pricing is used only to channel demand, not to inflate or suppress it. Fluctuating the price of a commodity allows a great deal of control: more, in fact, than the university or college may wish to have exerted on its users.

The success of any scheme in which users are responsible for correlating their use with financial reality finally depends on user access to complete and current information as to the status of their funds and usage. It does little good to tell a department chairman that the month before last his faculty and students have charged twenty-seven thousand dollars of computing to his annual six thousand dollar budget. For him to have any real control, the data must be current and complete. At one state college, for example, a single student for two months used 49 percent of the available computing, for a total of about thirteen thousand dollars before the accounting system was able to bring this fact to the attention of a responsible individual. Monthly and even semi-monthly status reports are generated at many colleges and sent to department heads, with a summary of the relevant departments sent to each dean. Such reports indicate current use, accumulated use, and remaining allocation. Some large centers have created on-line data bases containing this information, updated in real time, as the funds are being spent. Anyone who wants to know the status of his account can gain access to it by running a short computer job. At the University of Colorado, accounts are maintained to the level of the individual student. But it costs the student about forty cents of his allocation to query his account.

The control of excess demand by means of priorities and pricing structures is one problem; doing something to make use of idle capacity when demand is too low is something else. It does happen that a computing center is not crowded with users jockeying for position at the card hopper. Perhaps the center was designed for a peak load that has not yet been reached; perhaps it was constructed in anticipation of large research contracts that did not materialize. Since a computer has a limited life span and since much of the cost is not in capital equipment but is the on-going expense of personnel, rental, and expendable materials, this is computing that is being wasted. Naturally people wonder whether they could not find some worthwhile application of this wasted resource. One should be able to allow students and faculty free access to the computer at these times, whether they have allocated funds or not—or at least to lower the price so that more use can be encouraged.

At the same time, however, the problem may be seen in a different light by the accountants. Since—to return to the situation at Hypothetical University—a million dollar investment was to have produced a million dollars of computing, no more, no less, idle time means a deficit. Rather than lowering prices or giving away the idle capacity, prices should be raised in order to assure that the actual users cover the cost of what they are using.

Should the computing director lower the price to make sure the resource is not wasted? Or should he raise it to make sure that his expenses are covered? The answer for many institutions is found in an off-campus source known as the "Office of Management and Budget Circular A-21." This document declares that any user with federal funds may not be charged more than any other user of equivalent service. The federal rationale is that there is no reason why the government should have to pay for its computing if free computing is available to others. Thus, some standard price is required for all computing. Because of the issue of idle computer time, the document has been much abused by academic computer providers and users. And little argument can be made against the facts: because of A-21 enormous amounts of computer time have been wasted that would otherwise have been put to useful educational purposes.

To be fair, it must also be pointed out that the argument in favor of giving away unused service is not applied to any other resource on the campus. The telephone system, for instance, has some of the same characteristics of the computing system: building for a peak load that is seldom realized, schemes to level the load and to plan for stability, and idle capacity that could be used in the service of education for almost no cost. Yet no one complains that the telephone company does not make its idle equipment and service available late at night for students without funds to pay the long distance charges. The telephone company may reduce its rates for night time calls so as to attempt to balance the load, but it cannot give the service away.

HOW MUCH MONEY?

When faced with deciding how much to spend for computing, an administrator may turn to statistics about what other colleges are doing. The data that exist are only partially satisfactory, however, largely because the latest published survey information on computer use in higher education is from the academic year 1969–1970. It is risky to extrapolate trends from that date or even to rely on reports of plans being made in that year because significant changes in federal funding policies have altered the computing situation considerably on many campuses. Also, even when the data are current, radical differences in accounting practices and definitions of terms make one unsure exactly what is being measured. Finally, some of the statistics represent averages among such widely divergent institutions that it would be a mistake to interpret these averages as significant common practices. In the face of such uncertainties, one may sometimes be tempted cynically to browse through the data until he finds the figures that will support a predetermined position. A more useful approach may be to ignore the data and call on a few comparable institutions and ask them what they are up to.

Still, a brief review of some of the figures will shed some light on the situation. What, to begin with, is the size of the budget generally? In the academic year 1969–1970, about 470 million dollars were spent on computing for higher education, including research, instruction, and administrative computing. The distribution of these funds among the two thousand or so institutions is obviously not equal. The amount an institution spends will depend on its size, the level of the highest degree offered, and whether the institution is public or private.

A large doctoral level university with enrollment over ten thousand is likely to spend one to two and a half million dollars a year. Bachelor level colleges of comparable size will spend only about two hundred thousand dollars, approximately one-tenth that sum. This is partly because the doctoral-level university will have much more funded research going on; but more is also spent on instructional computing and administration. Colleges at the associate level are similar to bachelor colleges, spending roughly comparable amounts. Public institutions also tend to spend more than private ones.

Research and administrative computing may fluctuate because of the style of the institution. Thus figures on computing solely for instructional purposes may be of more interest than figures for all three applications. Of the 470 million dollars spent for academic computing, 142 million dollars, about one-third, goes for instructional use. Table 1 shows the range of figures for different kinds of institutions. These are for moderate-to-large schools (2,500 to 10,000 students) and are averages for all schools in the category including those that use no computing at all.

### Table 1

|           | Public | Private |
|-----------|--------|---------|
| Associate | 46,000 | ....    |
| Bachelor  | 50,000 | 18,000  |
| Master    | 38,000 | 41,000  |
| Doctor    | 77,000 | 80,000  |

These figures do not seem out of line or surprising, except perhaps for the master-level institutions.

Another way to look at the instructional expenditures is in terms of the cost per student. The numbers are very small. Looking at a table exhibiting this figure by size, level, and control of the institution, 22 of the 32 figures displayed are $10 or less. The cost per student rises only at very small institutions (where the basic costs must be spread among very few users) and the doctoral level institutions (where research computing tends to be complex and expensive). In 1967 the report of the President's Science Advisory Committee recommended a national average of about $60 per student.

WHERE DOES THE MONEY COME FROM?

For the most part, money spent for computing in colleges comes from the federal government, from industry, and from institutional funds. During 1967, when the President's Science Advisory Committee documented the critical importance of computing for higher education and estimated a desirable expenditure of $60 per student per year, they also recommended that the federal government should support at least some of this expense. The report has been much admired by computer specialists and by people in the academic community generally, but it was largely ignored by its primary audience, the federal agencies which might have helped subsidize the growth of computing in higher education. Looking backward, some members of the panel that prepared the report suggest that it was perhaps too honest. It claimed such importance for computing and such a high cost for good computing and adequate service that people in government were dubious. Then, too, it appeared at a very bad time, when the government was interested in decreasing, not expanding, its contributions to higher education. The federal contribution, however, has been considerable. In 1969–1970, 17 percent of the support for computation in higher education came from the federal government. But federal support has been largely for research at the major universities. Although the federal component has been about 40 percent, the percentage varies sharply by type of institution, ranging from 7 or 8 percent at associate and bachelor level colleges to 50 percent and more at some doctoral level universities.

If we attempt to restrict the analysis to computing used for instructional purposes, the federal contribution is not at all impressive; few classes of institutions can claim as much as a 10 percent contribution. Since the federal contribution has been primarily from the National Science Foundation for research purposes (including, of course, some research in instructional methodology), the college emphasizing instruction rather than research has stood little chance of getting federal money to support its computer use. Most analysts will agree that this situation is not likely to change much in the foreseeable future.

In the early days of computers, the industrial contribution to computing in higher education took the form of liberal discounts to educational institutions acquiring computers. Several reasons prompted the manufacturers in this direction: the desperate need for trained computer personnel; awareness of the considerable market that education would eventually be and desire to capture a share of that market; the prestige of having their machines on university campuses. In any event, these discounts have in the past made up a sizeable portion of the computing budget at institutions of all kinds, because the manufacturers, unlike the federal government, made their subsidies available to all institutions for instructional as well as research use—although specifically not for administrative use, in most cases. However, these funds are drying up, too. Most manufacturers have reduced or eliminated discounts for educational purposes. The original need for the discounts has largely been met, while the manufacturers have also been affected in their actions by the implications of Circular A-21.

It thus appears that, whatever has been the case in the past, most institutions can expect little help from the computing industry or the federal government in the future. Money for instruction in and with computers has been coming, and will continue to come in even greater amounts and percentages, from the general educational budget of the institutions themselves (in 1969–1970, they carried 70 percent of the cost of computing).

Many a college president, having learned this, has wearily picked up his phone and started seeking a donor of capital funds for a computer. But the problem is not capital investment but the recurring expenses. Supporting computing is more like endowing a chair than buying a building or books for the library. What the campus computing center needs is an endowment, but few institutions have found the courage or the arguments to try for one.

Beside these major contributors, there are a few other sources of money to support the computing center. Few of them promise ever to be more than minor, however. Spare computing capacity can sometimes be marketed off campus. If this practice is followed, there are bound to be complaints of unfair competition from commercial service bureaus. When can a college legitimately sell services to a commercial customer? Usually, the administration requires that the computing center demonstrate some unique capacity before it is allowed to enter into this kind of arrangement, for example, some particular hardware or software, or the participation of university personnel, before its resources can be used by a commercial agent. In any case, reliance on this kind of support for more than a trivial percentage of the budget means a vigorous marketing activity, which is usually just not available.

Becoming a regional center by marketing to other colleges also may seem an attractive possibility. But this means increasing the capacity of the computing center, making larger investments, and thus taking greater financial risks. It entails more complex and difficult management problems and probably, in the long run, does not mean cheaper computing for the institution that houses the regional center.

Some departments have special sources of money called "dean's funds" or "special funds," to be used at the discretion of particular departments or schools, and over which the university-wide planning agency has no control. Some of these funds are likely to go into computing, but probably for the kind of computing that cannot be acquired on campus. They will go to commercial service bureaus or to large university computing centers and will only rarely be spent on campus.

The ingenious administrator will find other lacunae in the system where a few computing dollars can be found. For example, in 1969 University of Texas students collected money to buy their alma mater two teletype terminals to be linked to the on-campus computer.

All of this information is of little comfort to the average administrator, who must still ask where the computing money is to come from. Unfortunately, many institutions have insisted on treating computing as a special item in the budget, to be funded in an unusual fashion, rather than as an integral part of education, to be funded like blackboards and chalk and teaching assistants and telephones. The money for computing cannot always be tacked on to an already over-extended budget. It has to come from cutting out something else, once the budget can be inflated no higher. When an author reviews and revises his book, it is an evasion of responsibility simply to make it bigger and bigger. He is required to decide what he will cut out to make room for what is new. The same is true for the tools of education, including computers. If computers are as important as their advocates and users say, then they must be willing to give up something less important in order to get the computing they need.

WHERE DOES THE MONEY GO?

Thirty percent of the computing available to colleges and universities serves instructional ends; 32 percent is used in research, and 34 percent in administration. These figures are based on 1969–1970 survey data but have varied only slightly in several years. Like funding sources, the distribution of computing varies widely by type of institution. Instructional computing at a large public university at the doctoral level can be 15 percent or less of the total, whereas at the associate or bachelor level, it is more likely to be 40 to 60 percent. But the data do not reveal a very striking or wide variation between individual institutions within these averages.

Once obtained, computer funds are spent for hardware, materials, and personnel. Equipment accounts for 40 to 45 percent of computer center operating costs. This figure appears to have been decreasing slightly, since it was commonly estimated at 50 percent or higher some years ago. Personnel costs account for about the same percentage of the total computing budget as hardware costs. Supplies, space, furniture, and the like make up the balance. These figures are not significantly different in large versus small centers, or in academic versus administrative services, although at a small college with its own computer the real figures are usually difficult to find—personnel costs may be hidden because the part-time service of several faculty members is not listed as a computing expense, while the hardware cost may be buried because the computer was purchased outright and no depreciation appears in the budget. In no instance that I know of is software a significant part of the budget for an academic computer center. Most software used in the academic or the administrative center is acquired free from the manufacturer or from other institutions, or is generated on campus. In those few cases where money is actually being spent for software, it has not amounted to more than 1 percent of the budget.

CUTTING COSTS

Computing costs on most campuses have risen sharply since the first machine appeared on the campus. Is all the current expenditure justified, could the budget be cut without jeopardizing the intellectual life of the institution? Although the answer is probably yes, some colleges have decided that the question may not be worth asking. They believe that even if some computing money is wasted, other problems are more critical. Other institutions have found significant ways to improve the whole operation, creating cheaper computing or more computing for the same number of dollars: for example, Carnegie Mellon University reported cutting over one million dollars from the computing budget, ostensibly without degradation of quality. Their budget analysis began with a list of questions, three of which seem especially relevant to many universities and colleges: (1) If computers represent the ultimate in automation, why does the number of personnel continue to climb? (2) If computers are so complicated and so vital, why do we have so many low-skill personnel working with them? (3) When we pay for hardware and software, why do we have to add so many of our own personnel to make them do what we want? To solve these problems, Carnegie Mellon implemented some novel techniques: the machinery in the center was rearranged, closed circuit television and intercommunications were added to reduce the number of operations personnel; a small number of highly skilled personnel replaced the large operating staff (one systems programmer and an assistant instead of eight to ten computer operators per shift); equipment was purchased rather than leased (possible with well-planned equipment selection); and hardware maintenance was done within the university instead of being contracted for. Accounting functions were also instituted, making the users more conscious of costs and permitting the computer center to vary the price in order to control the demand.

Two Carnegie Mellon principles seem of paramount importance: selecting competent management and making long-range decisions.

"Competence of management is measured not only by technical qualification, but also by whether the individual understands, accepts, and can accomplish the objectives of cutting and holding costs to a minimum, while supplying the required services. There is no guide to the selection of good management which will supplement the shortcomings of upper level administrators who do not possess the basic knowledge to properly evaluate their computing management. In this case, outside opinions and assistance should be solicited, but with the understanding that if a proper evaluation of existing management cannot be made by an upper level administrator, then a proper selection of outside assistance is equally difficult" (*The Financing and Organization of Computing in Higher Education,* 1971, p. 55).

"Very few computing facilities are established to accomplish a short-run objective. Most instances of installing and developing a computing system to a normal, smoothly functioning, production level involve years of effort. Historically, time spans of most efforts exceed five years, with a system being replaced at about the time that it is becoming a stable operation. There are very few cases where this updating of machines and systems have been truly justified and thus a significant increase in cost is caused not only by leasing instead of buying, but also by the continual rework of applications and software systems" (*The Financing and Organization of Computing in Higher Education,* 1971, p. 56).

The Carnegie Mellon technique seems to have worked, but it called for skilled management and good communication between the technical and administrative personnel. Not all colleges have this raw material, while the institution that tries to save money without this investment may destroy what it is most trying to preserve: the quality of computing on campus. Personnel costs can be cut drastically at almost any computing center, with little noticeable short-range effect. Much of the personnel expense represents competence available in case it is needed, when individual users require help in understanding particular software systems, or when programmers must change a program that has unaccountably developed a bug. Without such personnel resources, users must be sent away unsatisfied. They can work around the bug, but the quality of the service has been seriously diminished. Money has been saved at the cost of providing less computing, or low quality computing.

### RESOURCES AND REFERENCES

Sharpe (1969) has written a major study, incorporating much theoretical and practical information. The reader may be particularly interested in the chapter "Pricing Computer Services," which includes a discussion of the A-21 policy document. Sharpe's analysis of the purchase versus rental issue is also excellent.

Federal policy with regard to academic computing has earned much attention. A good summary appears in "Campus Computers" (1969). Greenberger (1971) and Davis (1971) trace some of the implications. Kanter (1968) discusses the impact of federal policy on pricing and allocation.

Hamblen (1967, 1970, 1972) supplies facts on how much money has been spent for computers in education and what it has been spent for. The reader may wish to review the most recent of these surveys, paying particular attention to statistics about colleges about the type and size of his own. The President's Science Advisory Committee (1967) made specific recommendations that are still valid as standards and objectives.

Kehl (1971) has described the situation at one very large university center. The reports of the Colorado computing director seminars also include papers by Krueger (1970, 1971) on the financial management of computing centers.

The information in this chapter on the experiences of Carnegie Mellon University is drawn from a paper by two members of the university administration (Rowell and Rutledge, 1971).

# INSTRUCTIONAL
# COMPUTING

Although the computing management problems dealt with in the preceding chapters naturally concern the administrator, he realizes that they are, after all, secondary to instruction, research, and administration. As instruction is central to the college, serving instructional needs must be central to campus computing. In fact, for the small college and the poor college, improving the quality of instruction may be the only argument that justifies the expense and trouble of bringing computing to the campus. Individual professors wishing to integrate computing into their course work in physics, psychology, or linguistics should seek the advice of colleagues and refer to the growing number of relevant publications. (Some of these can be located by using the resources cited in the List of Organizations at the back of the book.) Since the issues are discipline-related, they cannot be treated here. However, general issues exist that concern the faculty member regardless

106

of his department and that are also of interest to the administration in its concern for the nature, quality, and cost of instruction. Administrators and faculty may ask: How can computers improve the quality of instruction in the traditional disciplines? How can we bring the experience of those who have preceded us to bear on the instructional methods of our college? How can computing be introduced to a reluctant or indifferent faculty? What does our college need to offer in the way of instruction about computers? This chapter attempts to throw some light on these questions.

### PROBLEM-SOLVING

In most instruction, computing is largely used as a problem-solving tool. In the sciences and in engineering courses especially, students are required to solve problems involving a considerable amount of arithmetic manipulation that has traditionally been done with slide rules, logarithm tables, and calculating machines. The computer is a powerful addition to this arsenal. With it, students can do their problems quickly, allowing professors to assign considerably more complex problems, an important consideration. Some sciences deal with real problems so complex that the textbook problems must be watered down to the point where they reflect only dimly real issues of the science. The student is thus given little idea of what a practicing physicist, chemist, engineer actually does and what the current content of these disciplines really is. The computer allows the teacher to offer the student more realistic problems, providing him with a better understanding of the science. Since professional scientists or engineers often turn to the computer for help, the student who intends to follow a career in these disciplines needs to be aware of this new tool.

### SIMULATION

Simulation techniques use the computer to model the behavior of different systems. This technique serves important functions in research and instruction. In the social sciences, for example, the system model provides a laboratory for investigating the potential impact of alternative events on a social system; a model of a national economy can help gauge the effect of different government policies; a model of the electorate can help evaluate a particular campaign strategy or the relative effectiveness of several.

In the physical sciences, too, laboratory simulations are used where they are more economical, less dangerous, or just more feasible than a real laboratory. In medical instruction, for instance, allowing a student to examine a patient, prescribe tests, and attempt to reach a diagnosis has considerable educational value. A computer can simulate the patient, saving a human being the indignity of examination by a class of neophytes. In some chemical experiments the elapsed time is too long for a student to carry out the experiment in a real laboratory. In others, the process may be too dangerous or the equipment and materials too expensive. In these cases, the logic of the process (but not the physical manipulation) may be modelled with a computer. Introductory courses in particular may place more emphasis on introducing the student to the logic of the experimental method and the skills of scientific deduction than on teaching him the skills of handling the equipment and materials.

Computer "games" are perhaps the most valuable use of simulation in instruction. Generally they involve simulating the total environment of a single human decision-maker (for individual instruction) or a group of decision-makers (for class instruction). The students attempt to achieve some goal within the restrictions of the environment. Schools of business administration have been major users of such techniques. The class may, for example, play the roles of several corporation heads competing for a defined market. Each is told his resources and the position of his company at the beginning of the session. He is free to alter corporate policy in order to enlarge his share of the market: Should he raise or lower prices? Modify his research effort or his advertising budget? The computer represents the marketplace: it accepts student input representing perhaps a quarter or a full year and reports back on their sales figures. The students are then able to refine their policies further and continue with the game. Those whose policies represent an understanding of the nature of the market prosper; those who do not, go bankrupt. Like the simulation for the medical student or the chemist, the computer represents for these students an analogy with the real world they are being trained for. They can experiment without involving large sums of real money and the lives of other human beings.

DATA BASE INQUIRY SYSTEMS

Another important instructional use of computers is the management and investigation of large masses of information. If an individual or an enterprise has a collection of information (millions of separate items, perhaps) and wants answers to questions about it, the computer is an invaluable tool. The social sciences especially use computing for statistical analyses of samples, surveys, census reports, election returns, reports of economic factors over a period of years, and so on. Instructing students in these statistical methods is an important application of the computer. In all disciplines information management is also essential in dealing with the accelerating growth of the literature. Computer-based bibliographic information systems have thus become a valuable tool of research and instruction.

One of the most versatile systems for the management of information is Dartmouth's Project IMPRESS, an attempt to develop a laboratory for social science research and instruction. It is oriented toward the manipulation of the survey data that so often form the raw material of social science research. The goal of Project IMPRESS is to give the undergraduate student ready access to the wealth of existing social science data, so that he will be able to examine them with considerable freedom. He is given a range of data bases, a convenient language for describing the information he wants, and interactive access via the computer. He is able with relative ease to deal with a large mass of data, such as returns of a presidential election or even several independent collections—perhaps surveys on the same question at two or more different times. Access to such information allows him to make analyses and investigate relationships; he might ask, for instance, for the distribution of political party preference in a given survey by race or by age.

The system thus represents a fairly flexible learning tool. An instructor can suggest questions his students may attempt to answer by conducting research on the available data. How much they learn depends on the ingenuity of the instructor's questions and on the ability of the students to find ways to make the computer work for them.

A third application is computer-aided instruction (CAI), a term which may include any method whereby a computer is used to abet student learning. However, the term often simply represents the techniques of drill and tutorial instruction, in which a computer interacts with an individual student. In a drill situation, the computer is infinitely patient, asking simple questions again and again until the student demonstrates his mastery of the material. In tutorial applications, the computer functions like a programmed textbook but allows a vastly more complex network of paths than a book can provide. Typically a dialog is set up in which the computer provides information and then asks the student a question to test his understanding of what he has just read or seen. If the student answers correctly, he proceeds to the next step. If he fails, further explanation is supplied and he is asked another question. Using the computer thus allows the author of the lesson to provide a flexible set of responses, some of them ingenious in their diagnoses of the learning problems of the student.

Both drill and tutorial techniques have demonstrated their effectiveness: they help students to learn and they also provide a wealth of material to the teacher and the educational researcher on how the student learns. But is CAI economical? Low level instruction such as these programs provide can be acquired very cheaply from human sources. As in automation anywhere, CAI must be cheaper or faster if it is to compete with manual methods. Because the computer is able to speed up the learning process, particularly if individualized CAI is compared with lock-step group instruction, CAI has been used in industrial and military training, where the cost of the student's time is part of the equation. In traditional education, however, the value of the student's time is usually not considered, making it difficult to demonstrate that CAI is cost-effective in the schools.

Current research indicates that effective, efficient CAI requires large numbers of students to amortize the developmental costs of the instructional materials and the hardware. The hardware for the individual student must in turn be cheap since it is impossible to supply each of a large number of students with equipment costing tens of thousands of dollars. Several current projects are working on these problems; PLATO IV, a project at the University of Illinois, is developing an ingenious, low-cost, flexible student terminal with TV rather than telephone communications. Simultaneous use of four thousand terminals would assure the economical operation of this system. Because of the large numbers of students involved, this kind of instruction is directed at primary and secondary education rather than at the college level. Community colleges, however, show considerable interest in using CAI for core and remedial courses.

Another research project is TICCIT, in which the Mitre Corporation, the University of Texas, and Brigham Young University are participating. Courses are being developed in mathematics, English, and computer science, while the hardware uses standard television receivers, video tape recorders, and a minimum of electronics. The developers admit that the cost of TICCIT instruction is still not competitive with the cost of conventional instruction at the college level, at least as long as no price is placed on the student's time.

RESEARCH

The line between research and instruction is often hard to draw. Some research applications are also instructional applications. Using computers to control laboratory experiments and analyze data is now fairly common. Insofar as instruction parallels these research efforts, the computer is also an instructional tool.

CHANGES IN INSTRUCTION

In many fields computers are first used to support an activity previously performed by other means. As users grow familiar with the machine and its potential, they discover that they now have the means of achieving their ends by a radically different approach. Because of the great shift in possibilities, they may even need to reconsider their goals, realizing that much of their past work had been constrained by a limited awareness of what was possible. Thus the computer not only leads to a revision of the means but to a reconsideration of the ends as well. This pattern is beginning to emerge in instructional computer applications, but only very slowly. Practicing teachers, even within the same discipline and at the same school, find it incredibly difficult to share experience and technique in instructional methodology. Also, in many disciplines no well-defined set of instructional goals and objectives exists that would allow intelligent restructuring of the curriculum. Yet it seems clear that the sociology student who uses the Dartmouth IMPRESS system to investigate existing data on his own is receiving different training from the sociology student who reads and hears lectures about the investigations of others. The Dartmouth student learns by doing rather than by example. He is probably better schooled in the method of his discipline than he would have been had he learned by conventional means, although there are perhaps weaknesses in his knowledge, too.

At the University of California, Irvine, Alfred Bork has been investigating some of these questions. In his Physics Computer Development Project he became aware that it might be possible to take a radically different approach to instruction in the strategies of problem-solving and the development of proofs. Traditionally, the student reads or hears in lectures elegant solutions to given problems. He may understand the solutions but has no idea how to create such intellectual constructs. He is not aware that the first person to have done it may have made guesses, taken intuitive leaps, made mistakes, backtracked, started again, worked both back from the answer and forward from the premises, fumbled, and made grossly illogical deductions. To teach this aspect of theoretical thinking, Bork has developed dialogs called "interactive proofs." The students may make guesses (and hence mistakes) and may use a variety of techniques. If the student appears at a loss, he can be given hints to help him along. If he cannot see the whole proof, he may be able to see parts of it. The tutor remains passive as long as the student is proceeding confidently, whether he is proceeding in the right direction or not. The student is not given any information unless he asks for it and is free to move in any direction he selects.

Bork's project has also experimented with programs that are (like IMPRESS) unstructured vehicles within which learning experiences can happen. Such programs are less detailed scripts (as with a CAI tutorial program) than they are carefully defined sets of possibilities which allow the student to explore independently the given realm without wandering outside it.

Such techniques threaten to alter radically not only the method but the content of instruction, narrowing the boundary between instruction and research, and changing the role of the teacher in the educational experience. This book cannot attempt to evaluate these techniques or even to guess at their ultimate acceptance in the academic community. Yet few who have seen how students learn with them are totally unimpressed. Many teachers and schools are committed to them as a valuable and realistic approach in higher education. And ultimately, the contribution of computer-aided instruction to education may be well worth its greater expense.

INSTRUCTION-CENTERED COLLEGE

Like computer-aided instruction efforts for the past decade, the projects cited (PLATO, TICCIT, PCDP) all promise breakthroughs that will affect students at every level, everywhere, very soon—but not today. Even the simplest uses of computers in instruction require new instructional materials and the presence of an aware and interested faculty. The small college, without the resources to develop new instructional programs, and the community college, with neither the personnel nor the facilities to engage in research, may still wish to involve students in computer use. But how is it to be done?

The small college may have several problems: it may be somewhat isolated; the faculty may be tradition-oriented; and the administration may not be interested in spending money on computers. Altogether there may be little pressure to apply computers to instruction. The community college may be larger but faces problems of its own. Its primary function may be training technicians, nurses, and policemen, not scientists, and the use of computers may be impossible unless they improve instruction in a concrete and measurable way.

Yet the small-college situation may be viewed in a totally different light. Faculty members who focus on instruction rather than research are often attracted to innovative instructional methodology. Younger faculty who have used computers in their graduate education want to introduce them to their students. The informal and accessible computer center at the small college makes it easy for the new user to find his way. Ideas, techniques, even computer programs can be borrowed from large institutions. And, at the large community college, the large number of students in introductory and remedial courses, combined with the lack of graduate students to provide cheap instruction, may make computer use financially attractive.

One element is crucial to move a college from a tradition-oriented stance to an innovative one: a few willing and interested faculty members. They in turn may be able to persuade the top administration to obtain computer service and to endorse it. A college can wait until these faculty members appear, or it can encourage their development by new appointments, by encouraging established faculty members to go to meetings within their disciplines on the use of computers in instruction, and by bringing available documentation to their attention and putting it at their disposal.

Not all the work, however, can be done at the small college. Some of the responsibility for bringing the advantages of computer-based instruction to the instruction-centered college must rest with research universities, state coordinating agencies, regional computer centers, and national agencies, all of which have greater resources for developing the necessary but expensive instructional materials. It is not enough to send the students to be enlightened by the presence of a computer on campus. New problem sets must be developed for student use; simulations and game materials must be developed, borrowed, or bought; ideas for interesting and successful learning techniques must be shared. One knowledgeable college president remarked, "The small college is software limited rather than hardware limited. We have to make better use of our human resources and we can't afford the development expense." Fortunately, some institutions are now looking for ways to share with others the resources they have developed. Many regional centers and state-wide agencies for coordinating computing hardware are also taking an interest in sharing the development and publication of curricular materials. Five such regional centers (Dartmouth, Iowa, North Carolina, Oregon, and the University of Texas) have recently begun a cooperative effort called CONDUIT to transport instructional materials over a wide area.

### INCENTIVES FOR INNOVATION

The greater availability of instructional materials was also a major focus of a study conducted in 1970 by Roger Levien and some of his associates at the Rand Corporation (Levien et al., 1972) for the Carnegie Commission on Higher Education. This study concludes that students must have broader access to economical computing and that the development of cost-effective computer instruction must be encouraged. Thus wider utilization of instructional computing must be simultaneous with its improvement. The study suggests that the most effective strategy for a balanced program of both utilization and development will be to encourage the natural growth of the system, in which individual colleges direct the rate of growth, rather than a forced development, in which a national agency makes decisions. But in order for natural growth to take place, there must be: a means of supplying computing and instructional materials to all colleges regardless of location; a means of payment for use of these services and materials; incentives for the providers of computing services; incentives for authors of instructional materials; and incentives for distributors to circulate the materials widely. The satisfaction of these criteria would create a market for instructional materials that would naturally be receptive to the interests that emerged among users, developers, and suppliers. Software development would achieve a status impossible in the current situation, in which it is, according to Levien, merely a "cottage industry."

Most instructional materials are currently developed by the individual teacher who generates materials for his own students. If his materials are good and other teachers learn about them, efforts may be made to apply the materials more widely. This, however, implies a further expense and nuisance for the developer. He will be expected to give demonstrations, to provide detailed documentation for other teachers to use, answer questions by mail and phone, and to be responsible if his programs fail to work when they are installed on some other computer. For all this, he receives no financial compensation and little of the professional reward he would earn by devoting equivalent effort to a research paper. In fact, some people interested in acquiring instructional materials have found that developers may publish a paper about their materials but are not willing to share the materials described in their papers.

Nor is there incentive for a third party to act as distributor, collecting the materials from the developers and making them available to others. Further, no provision exists for users, either students or institutions, to pay for instructional materials. Although some computer centers and users are now realizing that software is not always free, it would be highly unusual for one faculty member to pay another for the use of his instructional materials or computer programs.

The Rand report suggests that a marketplace with the well-ordered structure of the textbook industry is needed to encourage faculty members, individually or in teams, to develop useful materials because of both the status of authorship and the promise of financial rewards. Distributing agencies would be expected to verify and somehow standardize the materials and also to provide a means of acquainting prospective users with them: a role analogous to that of the textbook salesman. Since the entire structure depends on financial incentives, fees would have to be collected from the institution or department (following the example of the computer service itself or the books in the library) or from the student himself (as with the textbook).

For such a situation to develop cheaper, more effective materials than presently exist must be available widely and in competition with on-campus computing. They must be standardized so that they can be transferred easily. There must also be a means of equal access, such as the widespread availability of regional service or the use of standardized minicomputers. Finally, faculty, students, and administration must be amenable to the entire scheme. If the new materials improve the quality of education, the students should be satisfied. If it is economical, the administration should be content. And, although there may be an implicit threat in automating some of the functions of the teacher, faculty should find the system acceptable and rewarding.

To get this development underway requires an initial effort by government or private industry and by individual institutions. The Rand report projects that the system may take eight to twelve years to mature. Since the publication of the report, cooperative agencies for distributing available materials have appeared; faculty and administration interest in economical means of acquiring software has risen; and the availability of regional computing has increased. However, financial aspects of the system, regarded as so important in the Rand model, have not yet surfaced.

### INSTRUCTION ABOUT COMPUTERS

Since much of instructional computing entails having students write programs to solve given problems, they need to learn the basics of computer use. Some of them may want to specialize in computing. Others may simply want to understand what the computer can and cannot do, without wanting to use it for any particular purpose. Thus the need emerges for three different kinds of courses about computers: basic instruction in computer use; training for computer specialists; and survey courses to meet the needs of the general student.

Basic instruction, or service courses, may be provided at a small institution by brief noncredit classes offered by the computer center staff. Alternatively, the departments that want their students to know about the computer may teach the course themselves. An introductory science course, for example, may devote a few hours to teaching the students the rudiments of FORTRAN so that they will be able to use the computer in solving assigned problems. However, it generally becomes advisable to centralize these functions and offer courses such as An Introduction to Computers and Programming or Beginner's FORTRAN through a single agency. A course for credit may include teaching a generally useful language like FORTRAN, introducing some of the basic techniques of writing and debugging programs, and clarifying the general nature of computing.

At some institutions, the location of such a course has turned out to be a controversial matter. If there is no computer science department, should the courses be offered in the mathematics department? This will satisfy a number of departments, but probably not mathematics. If it is installed in the engineering department, the social scientists and others may object that the instruction focuses too much on hardware. Any department selected is likely to use examples and exercises drawn from its own repertory and thus alienate some of the students. And at one large state university, a number of departments have apparently discovered that teaching their own courses on computing is an inexpensive way of increasing the number of student hours spent in the departments. Thus they oppose the creation of a computer science program to compete with their service courses.

Usually, however, by the time the demand is great enough to warrant the establishment of credit courses, there is also a demand for more advanced course work in computer-related topics, making a computer science program the most reasonable way of handling the need. The program may be established within mathematics or engineering because these departments may have the strongest interest and they do not appear totally inappropriate. If the computer science program eventually emerges as a full-fledged department, it may be difficult to know exactly where it should be placed. It is certainly not a physical science; yet it would be Pickwickian to call it a social science. Engineering is probably where it belongs if engineering is considered broadly as an investigation of man-made structures. But computer scientists frequently object to being coupled with engineering because this is misinterpreted as a tacit identification of computer science with computer engineering. Not infrequently, universities have made computer science an interdisciplinary, nonschool department, hanging in limbo without a dean. It may then find itself with such associates as Black Studies, Comparative Culture, and International Study. Such special cases tend to be difficult to manage effectively and eventually they are likely to be pressed back into a more traditional mold.

COMPUTER SCIENCE

But the establishment of a computer science program or department presents some problems more important and difficult than where it should be located: What should it teach? Who should teach it? These questions are not unrelated. With a new and ill-defined discipline, what is taught is often more a function of what the faculty is able to teach than what the students need to know. Unfortunately, some computer science programs have been much too ambitious, with the college offering courses that no faculty member could teach, while new faculty could not be hired.

But what do students want and need to know? Enthusiastic computer specialists may be tempted to present a full range of courses conforming to the standard theoretical structure of the subject. (The standard computer science curriculum reference is "Curriculum 68," 1968.) This approach is highly theoretical and is allied closely with mathematics. It is offered at a number of universities, but any school tempted to emulate them should consider that the need for graduates of such programs is limited; the computer industry demands a large cadre of personnel with practical training but needs fewer people with theoretical training in the discipline of computer science. Further, the cost of producing an undergraduate major in computer science (not to mention a Ph.D.) is quite high because of the large amount of computing he uses in his course work. Finally, the requirements for faculty ability, experience, and training are high, while computer scientists trained to that level are still rare. Providing instruction at a more practical and modest level, however, is not so difficult. Most teachers of computer courses are not trained theoreticians of computer science. They are retooled mathematicians, psychologists, even philosophers. In the future, we may expect university graduates trained as computer scientists in college-level teaching, but we do not need to wait for that day in order to introduce students to computing.

As a pure science, computer science is concerned with the analysis and description of languages and information structures. Computer scientists are interested in computer programs such as compilers for languages, systems operation, and general-purpose information processors. They are not usually concerned with the application of computers to real problems unless the application is novel or difficult or tests some theoretical concept. A different orientation for an instructional program is applied computer science, concerning itself more with computer applications. One of the primary applications of computers which threatens to overwhelm the computer instructional programs at some colleges is its use in solving the problems of business administration.

Since business and management constitute the largest general application of computers, business schools are beginning to satisfy the real need for graduates with a broad and thorough understanding of computer use in management. The computer science department may not be able to satisfy this need; thus the business school may rightly argue that it must offer its own courses, at least beyond the most general introduction. Recently there has been an effort to persuade schools of business administration to develop programs to meet the need for personnel specially trained in the development of management information systems. (See "A Report of the ACM Curriculum Committee on Computer Education for Management," 1972.) They become systems and computer specialists within the business school curriculum. The next decade will probably see the emergence of such programs at some of the more innovative schools.

At the community college level some schools have been successful in training programmers and operators to satisfy the manpower needs of the community. However, care must be taken that these young people are not sent out with too narrow a specialty in a rapidly changing field. Too often, young people who find a ready market for their specific skills also find that they can lose their jobs just as easily when they are undereducated and unable to keep up with changes.

Training in computers makes special demands on the computing resources of the institution. In arguing that off-campus service is inadequate, many computer people insist that students need "hands-on" experience, that they have to be able to touch the computer in order to learn from it. Of course this is untrue if taken literally. But there is a grain of sense in the argument. While the computer science student does not need to be physically close to the hardware, he does need to be able to approach it logically. He must be able to investigate and use aspects of the system that ordinary users do not care about and that may be (particularly in large systems) so protected as to be invisible in normal use. In a supercenter, the software interface usually is so complete that it blocks investigation of the hardware. If the interface deliberately clouds the distinction between hardware and software, specialists refer to the computer as it is supposed to be seen by the user as a "virtual machine"; the user can act as though this machine is the real one and the system is able to adjust its resources to support this useful illusion.

But the computer science student may want access to the real machine, not the illusory one, and to the hardware, not the software. Thus the computer science department may need its own machine to satisfy at least part of its computing requirements. This will probably be a small one but it should allow the students to develop and modify software, getting their minds, if not their hands, on it. Since computer science students may also find it important to have access to a variety of computers, it would be valuable if they could spend some computing funds off campus.

The growing impact of computers on our lives has persuaded many institutions to offer basic computer literacy courses. The job of teaching the course usually falls on the campus computer scientist. He may first urge everyone to take Computer Science 1: An Introduction to Computers and Programming, only to find this approach does not work very well. The nonspecialist student finds it dull, pointless, and too hard. Despite the great fascination it has for people who work with it, the computer does not appeal to all students. Some of them cannot see the applicability of computing (at least at this introductory level) to the problems they think are important.

An alternative approach has been to create a course without the objectionable aspects of the first approach, especially the laboratory contact with computers and programming. Such a course, sometimes called "computer appreciation," surveys how computers are used, with examples of applications in business and banking, engineering, medicine, and so on. This tends to be more popular with some students, but the professor may have an uneasy feeling that he is really only presenting a travelog of the computing world.

Another approach focuses on the computer as a social phenomenon and uses the methods of sociology or anthropology under the title Computers and Society. Such courses discuss how computers and allied machines have affected human institutions and how they have raised questions of human goals and ethics.

Probably the best decision on content is that the course should cover a little of everything: an introduction to the technology, as thorough and deep as the students will sit still for; the methods and concepts developed in various applications; the impact of computers and automata generally on society, government, and individuals; and the role of agencies and the responsibility of individuals in the control of computing technology. The students are then in a position to consider some of the questions they have wanted to ask from the beginning but that they are now in a better position to answer meaningfully. These may include such questions as: What is the effect of computers on the quality of our lives? Will more computers mean more leisure? How can a democratic society plan its decisions and actions to enjoy the benefits of computer technology without accepting the disadvantages? What mechanisms for control exist or need to be created? What are the responsibilities of computer professionals and of the general public? Although highly inflammatory, these questions are important. The purpose of introducing the general student to the technology of computers and the nature of their use is to make it possible for the teacher to de-fuse these issues and for the students to discuss them in a meaningful way.

### RESOURCES AND REFERENCES

The literature on the management of academic computing is sparse, while on the use of computers in instruction, we have an embarrassment of riches. Perhaps the best place to start is with the proceedings of a series of conferences (*Proceedings of a Conference on Computers in the Undergraduate Curricula,* 1970; *Proceedings of the Second Annual Conference on Computers in the Undergraduate Curricula,* 1971; *Proceedings of the 1972 Conference on Computers in Undergraduate Curricula,* 1972). Each contains about fifty papers, arranged by discipline and containing examples of the application of computers to instruction in a wide range of fields. Blum (1971) has a similar wealth of material, but oriented more exclusively to science instruction. Lekan (1971) catalogs available programs in computer-assisted instruction.

From the literature on computer-aided instruction, I recommend Holtzman (1970), and a volume called *Computer Aided Instruction and Computer Managed Instruction* (1971), which is the yearbook of the British Computer Society and contains reports on American and European studies. Oettinger (1969) presents a different perspective from these two books, pointing out the difficulties that stand in the way of the general use of technology in education.

Briefer surveys are available in several excellent articles. Suppes and Morningstar (1969), Alpert and Bitzer (1970), and Cooley and Glaser (1969) are particularly recommended.

A good review of CAI economics is found in Kopstein and Seidel (1968). The discussion in this chapter of the economic production of good instructional materials draws heavily on the report of the Rand study (Levien, 1972); in addition, a briefer paper reports on some of the highlights of the study (Levien, 1971b) and a conference report (Levien, 1971a) presents some alternative viewpoints.

Project IMPRESS is described in Meyers (1969, 1970). PLATO is described in Bitzer and Skaperdas (1971) and Bitzer (1971). (The content of the two papers is identical; either one is recommended, but not both.) TICCIT is reported in Stetten (1971) and Judd (1971). PCDP is represeented in the bibliography by three articles (Bork, 1971a; Bork, 1971b; and Bork and Ballard, 1972). In my descriptions of this project, however, I relied primarily on several unpublished papers in which Bork pursues some of his ideas further than in these published sources.

The standard reference on education in computer science is "Curriculum 68" (1968). Finerman (1968) reports on a conference on graduate academic research programs in computer science. A good brief survey of current computer science education is provided in a group of articles in a special issue of the EDUCOM *Bulletin* (Fall 1972). Computers in schools of business has been the subject of several studies. The most important reference, however, is Ashenhurst (1972); an interested reader is best advised to begin with it and to use its bibliography for further guidance.

The ACM Special Interest Group in Computer Science Education (SIGCSE) is an important organization in this field; like the other special interest groups cited, the SIGCSE holds meetings and publishes a valuable bulletin.

The first references in this section were to the proceedings of a series of conferences on computers in the undergraduate curricula. This series will continue and thus represents a valuable resource. Unfortunately, since it has no permanent organization or home, I cannot advise the reader on how to get current information on its status and plans. However, with copies of the available proceedings and a little attention to the names in these, one should have little difficulty in finding someone to ask.

# 10

# ADMINISTRATIVE
# COMPUTING

The use of computing in higher
education is usually analyzed into three categories: instruction, research, and administration. The previous chapter dealt with computing in instruction. In research, computing is so technical and
so closely allied to the methodologies of the disciplines involved that
it lies beyond the scope of this book. Administrative computing,
however, involves several topics of enough general interest and importance to warrant discussion.

The history of the application of computers to administration is usually a history of a gradual coming to terms between an
old process and a new method. At first some members of the staff
are likely to see the computer as a potentially useful servant, a
cheap, efficient mechanical clerk that can be applied to keeping
records, balancing accounts, preparing statements, and sorting lists.
But when these adventuresome staff members start looking about

for more work for the mechanical slave, they find that there is really not a great deal such a stupid clerk can do. The tasks must be precisely defined and ordered, so that instructions can be given completely and simply; they must also be repetitious, requiring the same operation for a large number of records so that the single explanation will suffice for all. But in many offices, including those of colleges and universities, few jobs have these characteristics. Many of the procedures are riddled with exceptions; many are understood only by the few people who have been doing them since the beginning.

However, as members of the staff begin to have frequent contact with the computing system and its support personnel, their thinking may subtly begin to change. They may start thinking in terms of the information required to do certain jobs, of decisions based on the orderly evaluation of facts, and of more highly structured organizations for efficient decision-making. And as they move in this direction, the systems and computers move closely behind them, creating throughout the administration a highly organized structure and a carefully defined process. The computer thus begins to transform the administrative process.

The first application of the computer on a college campus is most likely to be in financial management because in its financial affairs the college resembles other enterprises more closely than anywhere else. Thus the applicability of systems and techniques developed in business and industry is apparent to the financial administration of the college. Also, the financial policies and procedures are likely to be the most orderly of any administrative area at almost any college. Accounting and auditing tradition, not to mention common sense, requires that fiscal records be maintained according to a precise set of standards. Finally, everyone knows that finance has to do with numbers and that computers are good at doing arithmetic. At larger institutions, the registrar may follow closely behind the comptroller in beating a path to the computer center door. The high volume of paperwork in his office makes some kind of automation necessary, so he seeks ways to apply this stupid but efficient clerk to registration, student record-keeping, and even admissions. Eventually the computer is applied to tasks throughout the administration, including finances, student services, personnel, academic services, facilities, and auxiliary services. These areas fairly well cover all the administrative bookkeeping the college is likely to do.

Still, many members of the administration are not affected by the advent of office automation. Deans and vice-presidents, department chairmen, trustees, chancellors, and provosts live in an environment that is highly unstructured and very rich in nonquantitative values. They have important decisions to make and they need information on which to make them. But they often do not view their efforts as a deliberate collection and analysis of information. They talk to many people and collect impressions and ideas; they do not consciously structure or evaluate these data; when the time comes to make a decision, they may feel they act intuitively, basing their decisions on a humanistic awareness of values and goals. When they are offered more precise information, they may doubt that it will be of any value to them.

STRUCTURE OF INFORMATION

The computer systems people, however, start going through this rich clutter and point out that the decision-makers are being irrational. Don't they want to know the facts? One day the system analysts appear in the president's office with a diagram similar to Figure 2. They explain that it is a model of the information management functions of the administration. At the bottom, the analyst points out, is the day-to-day manipulation of information in the form of countless slips of paper. Most of the employees of the administration are involved in performing these functions: invoices are fed in and checks come out; registration forms are put in and class schedules emerge; worksheets are transformed into payroll checks. These employees do not participate in management or significant decision-making. Their job is to follow the policy and procedures established by their superiors. When a situation arises for which no policy exists, they are expected to stop and ask.

At the next level, the manager controls and coordinates the work of the first level. He must see that it actually gets done, that old obligations are fulfilled, and that new obligations are fulfillable. He needs to know if the research projects are on schedule, if all

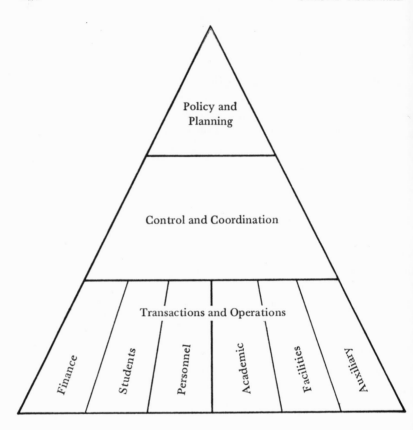

Figure 2

departments are maintaining their budgets, if the new building will be completed in time for fall classes, if the English department has found someone to fill its vacancy, and if the biology and chemistry departments resolved their office space conflict. To answer these questions, he must have the facts that pass through the hands of the clerks. Thus, while information passes *through* the operational and transactional level, some of it, abstracted and refined, should also pass *upward* as an input to control and coordination.

At the highest level, decisions must be made on how the institution is to be run and the direction it should be going. These are matters of policy and planning. The facts that influence these decisions are a further refinement of the information that is used at the middle level. The manager wants to know this month's income and expenditures so that he can assess the danger of overspending. The planners need a history of budgetary affairs rather than facts on the latest situation.

At this point, the diagram can be enlarged to include the information flow from the lowest to the highest level within the system and the flow into and out of the system as a whole, as shown in Figure 3. This diagram illustrates how information supports the administration. Of course, computers can be used to assist in the management of information at each of the three levels. In fact, the presence of computers eases the flow of information, particularly the upward flow.

TRANSACTIONAL SYSTEMS

At the lowest level of the diagram are systems that assist in the day-to-day manipulation of information by the administrative officers and clerks. As indicated, computer-aided systems may fall within the broad categories of finance, students, personnel, courses, facilities, and auxiliary services. In each of these, programs are developed to perform a range of functions, with each program supported by one or more files of data. Consider, for example, student record-keeping: programs assist in processing admissions applications, analyzing financial needs, processing registration, scheduling classes, keeping student accounts, reporting grades, and managing student housing. Files are maintained of admissions applicants, with details on their qualifications and the status of the applications; of current students, with background information (age, sex, permanent address) and academic information (courses taken and grades received); of students who are admitted but not currently enrolled; of ex-students who have not received degrees; and, finally, of graduates.

A diagram of the student record system at a medium-sized institution may look like a diagram of the Paris metro, for each file is related to two or more programs and each program is related to two or more files, making a richly interwoven network. The financial area also contains many programs and files, some closely interconnected. At one institution, an analysis of a single area revealed ninety-six separate computer programs routinely used.

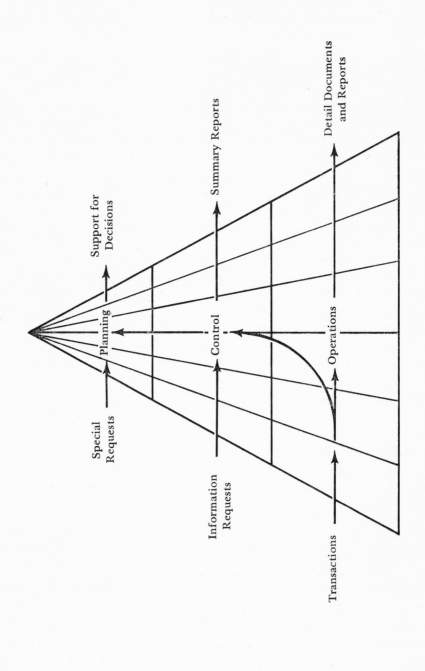

Thus, in each of the six application areas, a complex system emerges, with programs and manual procedures, computer-based files and manual files, input formats and reports. But note further that these six areas cannot be considered totally isolated from one another. Although they may think their problems are different, the comptroller and the registrar both maintain data about the same basic enterprise, so naturally their files overlap. The student record system contains data about student finances, relating it to financial records and programs. It has information about the student's academic career, relating it to files on academic services and faculty, the courses the students take, and the instructors from whom they take them. The faculty information is, of course, related to finances through the payroll. The facilities file is related to the academic services because the size of available rooms must be taken into account in assigning students to classes.

Although all the functions are related, this relationship is not necessarily reflected in the programs and files developed by different administrative offices. Different principles, different methods of coding and sorting will have been used, with no easy way available to bridge the gaps. But they need to be bridged if the data are to be used for more than the clerical functions for which they were originally created. To answer questions at the control and coordination level, information is required that demands inputs from more than a single file. An analysis of the cost of instruction, for example, may need information about students, courses, faculty, finances, and facilities.

When a college realizes the need for building bridges between files, it may be ready to develop a second generation of systems with a broadly planned base. The needs of users throughout the college are considered. In deciding on the format and content of the student record file, the special needs of the library, the food services, housing offices, the student loan officer, and the institutional research office, all have to be taken into account. This means, of course, that the file will probably become much larger and more cumbersome than it was because it contains data for many purposes. It also means that the system design effort is going to be difficult, time-consuming, and expensive. But it must be done if the data acquired in the transactional functions are to be used for the operations closer to the peak of the triangle.

Control and coordination at the middle level usually mean generating reports as a natural adjunct to performing the transactions at the lowest level. When the checks are written and debits to accounts made, a report on the status of the budget is also prepared. When registration procedures are complete, a report is generated on how many students registered, how many credit hours are being taught by each department, and so on.

Planning and policy, however, require broader and longer-range sets of information than needed for control and coordination. Rather than current budget status, planners need a review of the change in budget patterns by categories over the past ten years. Rather than data on this semester's registration, a report is wanted which predicts on the basis of historical trends the number of undergraduate majors in each department over the next five years.

To support planning and policy-making, several specialized computer programs are useful. One is the simulation program, which sometimes assists administrators in predicting the effect of closely interrelated factors. Not infrequently, a decision must be made on matters with complex and far-reaching implications: instituting a new program, for instance. Some decisions are made by others: students move away from some programs, while other programs gradually become popular. These decisions also have complex impact. Higher enrollment in a nursing program, for example, has an impact on many departments since nursing students are more likely to take courses in biology and chemistry than in economics or French. Some computer models are helpful in assessing the loads on various departments and the consequent costs. The Resource Requirement Prediction Model (RRPM) developed at WICHE is a good example. It basically takes student enrollment projections and converts them to the resources necessary to support them: these projections are then evaluated in terms of cost. Another well known and widely used model is called CAMPUS and was developed by the Systems Research Group of Toronto. It accepts inputs describing the structure of the college, academic programs and policies, enrollment, staff, facilities, and space. On these bases, it projects student flow, faculty load and teaching space, and the impact on support resources (such as the library). Finally, forecasts of costs and revenues are made. With such a model, alternative plans and policies can be assessed in terms of their resource implications.

Some administrators have the impression that these tools are highly sophisticated and only useful to the large university. This is not true. Small colleges have made admirable use of modelling techniques, sometimes with remarkably simple programs. Budgets for the next few years can be forecast on the basis of estimated future enrollments, faculty salaries, student-faculty ratios, endowment or tax yield, and so on.

The quality of a simulation depends primarily on the degree to which the model functions like the real world. Sophisticated models like the two cited above also require a considerable amount of reliable data on what the college is like now and what it has been like over the recent past. The more accurate the description of the situation is, the more detailed the predictive possibilities of the model are. Models are not crystal balls and have no more ability to foresee the future than the people who build them and use them. But where systems are very complex (and today's college is certainly such a system), they can help to evaluate a possible course of action and its implications for the system as a whole.

Some college administrations may be interested in a management information system. This system consists of (1) detailed current and historic information about the operation of the institution and (2) programs for retrieving facts and answers to questions from this data base. The data base includes information accumulated from the operation of transactional systems over a period of years. The programs allow for the organization and management of the data and for fast, cheap, and convenient means of getting needed information out of the data base. It may be very useful to know, for example, how the characteristics of the average student have changed over the past five years or what relationship exists between a student's academic performance and the size of the high school he attended or what the effect is of dropping out for a year. A management information system is designed to make it easy to find answers to questions like these.

However, such information systems are complex and expensive and are worthwhile only if the information obtained is worth the considerable cost of developing and maintaining it. Few universities can claim to have a complete management information system, although the concept of maintaining historic information in usable form is growing in acceptance. When information is understood to be a substance of value, with an effect on the success and efficiency of the organization, it is worth some expense to develop and maintain.

But information is not in itself valuable, despite its great and growing popularity; how it will be used is the key to its value. In their zeal to improve the quality of information available to administrators, systems people sometimes overlook the limits to the amount of it that the administrator can actually use. Such analysts are improving the quality of the input without assessing the ability of the system to absorb it. When the system does not improve, they may then consider that it is the people who are at fault and throw up their hands in despair. Making the people better processors of information is a far more complex and difficult task than the analysts may be able to tackle.

One frequent visitor to college and university campuses has found the answers to a few stock questions good indicators of the information quotient of administrators. For example, in talking to a registrar, he asks how much it costs to produce a transcript. Answers have revealed three levels of information capacity and management sophistication. Most registrars do not know what it costs to produce a transcript, in itself no great lapse. Any competent analyst or office manager can find this number in a few hours if he is told what to do. A registrar need only direct someone to get the data or get it himself. But many registrars do not know how to find out what a transcript costs them. Of course, they are academic officers and not technicians; they are not expected to know everything. Any competent management consultant could tell them how to get the information. They can pick up the phone and ask someone if they want to know. A disturbingly large number of registrars, however, do not know what it costs, do not know how to find out, and, further, do not understand why anyone would find this number interesting or what they would do with the number if it were given to them. No one in the registrar's office, no consultant or technician, can help such an administrator since he does not know what information is for, at least in this particular case. He is likely to justify his indifference to the cost of transcripts by saying, "It's a service the college is obliged to perform, don't you see, no matter what it costs."

But, one may ask, if you don't know what it costs now, how can you evaluate possible improvements? And how can you set the price of a transcript without knowing if the price is only a nuisance fee or if you are gouging the students? "Ah," says the registrar, "I am sure we are not cheating the students. It takes a great deal of time, you see. The girl who handles the transcripts waits until she has a stack of requests to do, and then it takes her most of a day to get them run off and mailed out." How often does she do this, and how many hours make up most of a day? "Why, she does it as often as she needs to, and most of a day is all the time she can spend, considering her other duties."

And so it goes. He cannot supply quantitative answers to questions because he does not really think in terms of quantitative information. Small wonder he cannot make use of more of it. When the computer consultant recommends a management information system that will inform the staff about the way the college functions, in great detail and in terms of quantitative data on actual performance, what use will it be to this registrar? He has reached the limit of his ability to generate, use, and absorb management information. If better information is to improve the management of the college, the improvement process must begin inside the head of the registrar and not with his files and office procedures. He is like a program with a bug in it; the program produces garbage no matter what its input, as long as the bug remains. The registrar can not use information unless he learns how to be a totally different kind of manager. And this is not the job of the computer analyst or the management consultant.

What, one is then tempted to ask, can be done for him? The question assumes that a change is needed and that anyone who does not have a continuously growing information appetite needs retraining. This may be true but there is another possibility. Perhaps the registrar, despite his failings, is operating at an adequate level of efficiency now. Perhaps increasing his information quotient and changing his method will do nothing but unsettle registration and make the whole process more expensive. If registration goes on year after year, grades get reported, and transcripts get duplicated and delivered without error, the system probably works well enough.

However, if the administrator is not performing his job well, some change in his style of management may be called for, even at the risk of expense and hurt feelings. Where can one begin? The biggest hurdle is convincing the administrator that there is something he needs to learn. Probably no one can tell him this but the president of the college. He has likely been in his position too long to accept such criticism gracefully. But if he accepts the challenge, there are ways to proceed. Management consultants can then teach him how to use quantitative information to do his job better and more easily.

He should be stimulated but not frightened. New ideas must be presented as an intellectual challenge. He must see the new methods as a way of making his job easier, not as a means of making it easier for the president to see his mistakes. He must be led and not prodded. He is probably far too clever to allow himself to be pushed into what he thinks may be a corner.

He may be using his day-to-day crises as a means of escaping his long-range duties. Can he state the real objectives of his office and their relevance to the goals of the institution? If he is really too busy with crises to tend to his long-range responsibilities, the first order of business, of course, is to provide him some help so that he can alter his priorities. Once he is willing to learn and has the time, visits to the registrars of other, more progressive institutions may be the best vehicles of enlightenment and persuasion.

Some cases are insensitive to any of these treatments. A fairly drastic step that sometimes helps is hiring a bright young assistant, who may inspire the older man to learn some new tricks. If the registrar remains unimpressed, at least this device trains a replacement. For if all else fails, the classic method of improving academic administration must be employed: the college must wait until the old registrar retires.

COST, EFFECTIVENESS, AND COST-EFFECTIVENESS

Although some institutions may have only marginal use for information systems, other colleges and universities of all kinds and sizes are creating, using, and maintaining information systems. As one might expect, the size of an institution is an important factor in the use of computer-based systems. The very large institution today finds it almost impossible to perform its transactional functions without computers. A review of administrative computing from 1965 to 1970 (see Table 2) reveals the importance of size. However, the steady increase of computing in colleges, is impressive and indicates the growing importance of information for administration everywhere. But in many institutions the use of computers may well be as much a function of the state of mind of the administrators as of the size of the student body or the budget. Colleges with well trained, aggressive, young administrators are likely to value information highly and to bear the cost of computer-based systems willingly.

*Table 2.* Percentage of Institutions Using Computers in Administration—Source: aacrao Surveys, 1965, 1966, 1967, and 1970.

| Size | 1000 or less | 1000– 5000 | 5000– 10000 | 10000– 15000 | 15000– 20000 | 20000+ | Total |
|------|------|------|------|------|------|------|------|
| 1965 | 9.8 | 36 | 79 | | 86 | | 31.5 |
| 1966 | 7.3 | 40.5 | 83.4 | | 96.1 | | 40.1 |
| 1967 | 11.5 | 44.5 | 88.2 | | 95.4 | | 41.4 |
| 1970 | 28.4 | 69.3 | 93.3 | 97.6 | 100 | 100 | 61 |

A likely question when a college first considers the acquisition of a computer-based system or whenever a change is contemplated is "What will it cost?" or even "How much money will it save us?" This is very often the wrong question and perhaps should not be asked at all. George Turner, director of information systems for the University of California, states, "Almost every system we have built is more expensive than the one it has replaced because we collect more data and generate more reports." Few administrators who have developed systems to help them in their jobs can claim a reduction in cost even at the transactional level. They are much more likely to claim an improvement in service. Even when systems are undertaken primarily for financial reasons, they are likely to end up costing as much or more than the manual systems they replace, but providing much more useful information.

Yet costs must be considered, after all. No matter how much a system does, the price tag may be too high. No matter how much information a system provides, no matter what the intangible benefits in terms of good planning and wise decision-making, many institutions will find the cost of a complete, integrated, effective management information system totally outside the realm of the possible. One private university has just completed work on a major system, integrating all its administrative systems and allowing for a flexible management information component as well. One of the men responsible for its development suggests that this is the last system that this university will ever be able to develop. Even for a large and relatively wealthy institution, the cost of going any further is out of the question. The ultimate returns from more and better information may be potentially great, but the cost is simply too high, for as systems grow in sophistication, flexibility, and universality, the costs grow as well. Having a sophisticated system means hiring and keeping a large highly skilled staff to create and maintain it. The more sophisticated the system becomes, the more the software and the people will cost. Although everyone knows that the cost of computers is going down and down, the cost of the army of people required to use them goes up and up.

COST REDUCTION

What can be done to drive the cost of systems down to the point where institutions can afford good information? At many institutions, the high cost of personnel is combated by using student help for programming and even for system analysis tasks. But some administrators have found out to their sorrow that this saving has a price. Students do not have much background in systems. Although they may be ingenious programmers, they do not regard their association with a programming project as their primary activity or responsibility, and they rarely stay more than a few years. The experience they lack must be made up by the manager who guides their activities. He must review their work carefully, insisting on detailed and accurate documentation so that if the student leaves his job suddenly, someone else can pick it up.

Another alternative is to ask an outside contractor to do the systems and programming, thus avoiding the cost of hiring personnel. The cost can be further cut in some cases if the contractor is allowed to market the system elsewhere. This is an attractive possibility and has been used successfully by a number of institutions. But there are dangers here too. First, the institutional representatives should be sure that the college and the contractor agree on basic principles. They must be satisfied that the contractor is competent and can work in the environment of academic administration, which is different from other kinds of offices. Both should be aware of the need for user participation in every stage of design, development, and testing, so that the ultimate system reflects the needs of the college. Finally, the college representatives should see that adequate time is allowed for parallel testing of the new system with the old one, to be sure that there is no hiatus between the two. One college president claims that after accepting a new financial system, "for six months, we didn't know where our money was!"

COOPERATIVE VENTURES

It is bound to occur to some people that one way to cut the cost in half is to double the use made of the system. If two colleges use the same system and share the development cost, they have saved 50 percent. If more colleges cooperate, the savings will be correspondingly greater.

Unfortunately, this is only partially true. Cooperation is never as easy as it looks. A system for two users, unless their requirements are identical in every detail, must have greater generality and flexibility to serve them both. These characteristics are not free; they imply complexity and its attendant cost. Successful administrative systems are difficult to accomplish at all; increasing their complexity and generality makes them more difficult still. Further, when several institutions cooperate, it is also necessary to establish procedures for central maintenance and on-going modification and improvement. The communication among the colleges and the necessarily high level of documentation also add to the cost.

If such a venture is to succeed, it is necessary that the co-operating colleges first have similar philosophies and goals with regard to the projected system. Two institutions cannot have a common registration system if they have different attitudes about the importance of a student's freedom of choice in such matters as time of day and instructor. Private and public colleges will probably have different financial reporting requirements. To create systems adequate to the divergent needs of such different institutions is probably not possible.

Second, the colleges must be more or less at the same stage in their use of computers and their appetite for information. Lack of similar experience is proving to be a stumbling block in the development of unified systems for one group of state colleges and universities. One of the institutions has experience with a highly developed system, but it would be totally inefficient to install a system of this complexity and cost in all the colleges, since most of them have little use for this level of information. But if a simpler system is developed, the sophisticated institution will be constrained to move backward and give up some of the management skills its administration has developed.

Finally, there must be some common definitions and standards. The institutions must have the same idea of what constitutes a student and of how space is to be defined; they may even be required to have the same chart of accounts or at least some basic similarity in their accounting systems. The National Center for Higher Education Management Systems (NCHEMS) has been responsible for giant strides in this area by supplying some basic definitions of common information terms. But the management systems of colleges of different size and type are still incompatible over large areas.

The development of regional computing has encouraged people to think of shared administrative systems, as it has encouraged the development of shared instructional software. In New Jersey, for instance, the state-wide computer service has developed administrative systems and made them available to the colleges by means of the central facility. The colleges are not constrained to use these systems. However, they do perform the functions most of the colleges need and they do prepare the mandatory state reports in the proper format; thus they are designed to appear convenient to the colleges. Florida also developed a central computing facility with a concentration on administrative systems. Groups of system users from many campuses are convened to establish requirements with the aid of professional system analysts. In Florida, in fact, the development of such common systems preceded the concept of a common computer facility for administrative purposes.

Whether cooperative systems are developed voluntarily or at the initiative of a state-wide office, the problems cited above must be considered. In creating a state-wide information management systems, however, there is an additional obstacle. Some administrators are uneasy about creating a situation where information is easily and widely available. A common computer system may be a threat if it appears that a college's internal accounts and statistics will be available to off-campus agencies without the knowledge of the college concerned. If a system at the state level is to be acceptable to a state college (or at the county or municipal level to a community college), there must be some guarantee that the data created by the system for the college is not available to off-campus agencies except through the on-campus administration.

Thus many difficulties arise in creating and living with systems developed for more than a single institution. But with the rising need for information and the growing cost of sophistication, there seems little other direction in which to move. Few colleges can afford to create systems that exactly match the style of the current staff in its current stage of sophistication. The soaring cost of systems means that most colleges must turn from custom-built systems to ready-made ones, learning to accept some discomfort and inconvenience.

### MODELS FOR FUTURE DEVELOPMENT

But the situation cannot possibly be as grim as this seems to suggest. Surely there are a few colleges that share virtually identical requirements for payroll or admissions form processing. It is hard to believe that there is a need for more than two thousand distinct student record formats adequate to justify the expense. And surely, someone has already produced a system basically similar to the one we are about to start on.

An organization called CAUSE (College and University Systems Exchange) has begun an ingenious effort to publish the wide range of options currently open. CAUSE catalogs and describes existing computer programs that appear to be transferable and that the developers are willing to share. Using this catalog, members can locate systems close to what they want, request documentation for further study, and, if the entire system cannot be used, then at least to borrow ideas. Finally, if the documentation reveals that the system may be acceptable, copies of the computer programs can be requested.

Many commercial agencies have produced programs for many administrative applications and offer them for sale or lease. It is hard to comment in general on these. Often they were developed for use by a particular institution and the developer retained the rights to market the product elsewhere. Other systems have been developed speculatively to serve the needs of a wide range of colleges. A particularly attractive and successful system may be taken over by a hardware manufacturer from the college that developed it, generalized somewhat, and documented, so that it can be made available to other colleges using the same computer. The National Center for Higher Education Management Systems has developed programs, too. However, these are at the policy-planning rather than the transactional level. The RRPM simulation, mentioned earlier, is the best known of their systems.

In considering how future trends may affect the alternatives of colleges in sharing the costs of administrative systems, it is useful to consider some of the components of these alternatives. There are, first of all, several possible models of development. A system may be developed: by one institution for its own use, then modified and installed at another; by one institution for its own use, but with generalizability as a secondary requirement; by several institutions as a cooperative project; by an independent party with no particular institution in mind, but with consideration of a wide range of requirements. An institution may accept a system on its own merits or because it is imposed or at least strongly recommended by some higher authority (such as a state board) that will profit from conformity on the part of individual colleges. There are, further, several ways a system can be arranged with respect to hardware: all users share the same hardware at a regional center; users have independent hardware but it is all of the same basic type so that few compatibility problems occur; the system is developed in a language adaptable to any computer with relatively little expense; reprogramming may be necessary to install it on a second computer.

It is not difficult to fit existing systems into the matrix defined by these three sets of alternatives. Financial systems offered by banks and commercial service bureaus, for instance, are developed independently, are accepted voluntarily, and are run on a centrally located facility, although it is not strictly speaking a regional center. Colorado's CHESS system was based on the concept of similar computers at all institutions, voluntary use, and single campus development of the programs. RRPM is an independently developed system that is available in hardware-independent form. Since Stanford's complex OASIS system was developed with a secondary requirement for generalizability, other universities with similar computers can use it with only minor reprogramming.

It is not feasible at this time to try to predict the kind of model that will best encourage the development of high quality administrative systems. All the avenues indicated by these dimensions or alternatives will probably continue to be explored and the concept of generality and the techniques of transference will be expanded and improved. But we can be sure that some form of cooperative system development is essential as systems grow more complex and more expensive; and as more cooperation takes place, more will be learned about how to do it.

RESOURCES AND REFERENCES

The literature of data processing in business administration and in management information systems is large since data processing for management is one of the largest application areas for computers. I will not touch on this literature here; numerous bibliographic sources are available for those who wish to look into it.

The literature of computers in academic administration is much more modest. But several valuable references belong in the library of any interested administrator. Very general materials include a brief paper by Farmer (1971) that gives an excellent introduction to the subject. The Rand report (Levien, 1972) contains a chapter which surveys the field. Johnson and Katzenmeyer (1969) have edited a collection of papers that includes some general philosophic presentations and some specific analyses. It is a valuable book and well worth reading. Another collection of papers that gives a good overview is Minter and Lawrence (1969). This is the report of a conference but consists of fairly formal papers. It also contains a very good bibliography (although only up to 1969, of course).

Detailed descriptions of specific programs and systems will be of value to some readers. I will not give any specific references on this topic because the field is so broad; it is more valuable to give some leads on where to find what you are looking for. The *Journal of Educational Data Processing* covers computer use for all purposes at all levels of education but has published a number of good papers on administrative applications in higher education. CAUSE, as described in the text, has begun to maintain an index of available systems. It would be a good place to start if one is looking for some program descriptions in a particular area. An organization not mentioned here before is the College and University Machine Records Conference (CUMREC). It is a series of meetings (since 1956) rather than an organization with a year-round function. However, it now has a permanent office to which inquiries can be addressed. The meetings attract people largely from administrative data processing, which is reflected in the papers and published proceedings. The American Association of Collegiate Registrars and Admissions Officers (AACRAO) has conducted periodic surveys of administrative applications, the most recent of which is included in the bibliography (1970).

Donahue and McKinney (1970) are an important source on information systems. Although written in a dry, textbook style, their analysis is crammed with information.

The use of models in administration is discussed and the RRPM and CAMPUS are described in two books already recommended (Johnson and Katzenmeyer, 1969; Minter and Lawrence, 1969). A reader wanting more details on the models and their applicability to his own situation should contact the agencies marketing these models for further technical documentation. An interesting paper on the use of a model for a small four-year college has been written by the president of such an institution (Prentice, 1971).

*Computing in Higher Education* (1971) discusses computer systems for university planning and includes information on the difficulties of using information systems. The most active organization in this field is the National Center for Higher Education Management Systems (NCHEMS), which makes its home at the Western Interstate Commission for Higher Education (WICHE). Since NCHEMS continues to publish interesting and useful documents, it is worthwhile keeping informed of what they are doing. I have included in the bibliography a paper that describes the history and goals of the organization (Lawrence and Gulko, 1971). A final reference is Hefferlin and Phillips (1971). It does not deal with computers or data processing specifically but it has a lot of useful advice on publications, meetings, consulting services, and so on.

# 11

# ACQUIRING
# SYSTEMS

The wise administrator leaves technical questions to the technicians and does not become involved in discussions of matters beyond his technical depth. Yet occasionally technical issues arise that require comprehension and decision at the highest levels of academic administration. These issues usually concern the acquisition of major hardware or software systems requiring a large financial investment, a long-range commitment of the college to a specific plan of action, and the cooperation of several different interests on the campus. Thus it is appropriate that the decisions have the attention, comprehension, and participation of many people on the campus, including members of the administration up to the president.

This chapter discusses the acquisition of hardware and hardware services for a general purpose computing center and the design and implementation of software for administrative systems.

A college with an established computing service also has a vehicle for bringing the need for more computing to the attention of the college. Symptoms appear that lead members of the policy committee or user group or the computing director to suggest that it is time to expand the service. At a college where no organized computer use exists, the symptoms are subtle and must wait for recognition until an administrator, faculty member, or student asks why there is no computing. At this point, a committee can be organized to look into the question.

*Defining need.* In either case, a formal group is set up to review and document current and expected use. The group accumulates data on current use (by whom, for what purposes, etc.), by type (along the lines sketched out in Chapter Two), the trends of usage over the past few years, the situation in comparable colleges, and probable future developments. Their report includes special notes on areas that may expand quickly: interactive student use, perhaps; or anticipated changes to the administrative system.

It has certainly been a major theme of this book that documents like this one, which may be called a requirements analysis, are not to be technical reports couched in the jargon of the computer. Its function is not to announce what members of the computing establishment would like to have, but to give a wider readership some understanding of the role and importance of computing in the life of the college.

Eventually, the series of committees, discussions, visits, and reports results in a recommendation with a pricetag on it. The documentation must enable nonspecialists to associate this pricetag with the instructional, administrative, or research value of computing for the college. This had better be done here, right at the start, before it gets lost in the details and urgencies of later phases of activity.

It may be unrealistic to ask the committee for a totally documented demonstration: a large computer is the only means of achieving certain objectives and is the most economical means of achieving others. But it is not unreasonable to expect the committee to consider the importance of computing to the college as a whole. In an attitude of financial realism appropriate to today's college administration, the committee should indicate an awareness that computing is not an "add-on" budget item; money spent for computing is usually money not spent for something else. Since computing does not serve every member of the community equally (few resources do), spending general funds for it must be justified.

Even this early in acquiring a computer or a service, a documentation of requirements probably indicates much about the college's attitudes on computing: whether the college intends to spend the minimum it can get by with, for instance, or whether it intends to push computing on people to the limit of their ability to accept it; whether the source of this intent is in the administration or in the faculty or whether (as sometimes happens) the computing director is documenting the use he would make of the computer if he were faculty and administration.

*Evaluating alternatives.* Assuming it is possible to document a real need for computing, the consideration of alternatives for satisfying this need is clearly the next step. The committee should compile a catalog of available services in the area, along with estimated costs; estimate the future impact of regional or national networks; consider the use of mini-computers for subgroups of users; and so on. No requirements analysis justifies the conclusion that the college must buy a new computer, even though this jump is made at some college every day. The richness of alternatives and their effective utilization by colleges of all types and sizes indicate the importance of considering alternatives to buying hardware.

The larger college or the university with a considerable research budget usually finds itself selecting a combination of services. Mini-computers are used in scientific laboratories and other isolable uses with special requirements. Some services are probably acquired from off-campus sources. In addition, an on-campus center serves such users as students, the administration, and certain research applications.

But the smaller college is not usually able to solve its dilemma by buying a little bit of everything. Its limited resources can buy only one of a small number of alternatives, such as a moderate-size on-campus computer for all users; off-campus services from a regional center or commercial vendor, or both, for all users; or separate academic and administrative use, serving each with a small on-campus computer or off-campus service. The only complex option is the acquisition of a small computer that can process much of the work and also serve as a vehicle for communicating with a larger computer located elsewhere, probably at a regional center.

Since the college's choice from among these options probably cannot be undone or modified for several years, it is important that it be based on the two documents described above: an analysis of need and an analysis of the available alternatives. And, in these documents, perhaps the two most critical issues to be resolved are the relationship between academic and administrative use, and the importance of interactive as opposed to batch computing for all purposes.

*Request for proposal.* At many institutions, the analysis of alternatives results in the decision that some hardware must be acquired for on-campus installation, either a freestanding computer (that is, one that processes all jobs submitted) or one that also serves as a remote job entry to a larger computer elsewhere. In some cases the decision about proceeding from here is easy. If, for instance, the plan is to expand the current facility with compatible hardware, the options may not be many. If the hardware must be compatible with that of a regional center, this requirement also limits the options.

In most cases, however, the market provides at least two alternative pieces of machinery for the job. Academic institutions have probably wasted more money by neglecting this fact than by any other decision about computers. In their haste to avoid any display of indecisiveness, colleges often ignore most of the alternatives and invite a single vendor to submit a proposal. Men who would not consider buying a car or a house without shopping around often invest college money in what a single salesman tells them is the wisest choice.

Talking to only one salesman certainly simplifies and accelerates decision-making. But it is an expensive luxury. The alternative is to write a request for proposals, accept and evaluate proposals from several vendors, and possibly end up with a complicated but economical hybrid that includes a central processor from one manufacturer, memory and peripheral devices from another, and software from yet another agency. Many colleges claim with some justice that they do not have the time or the technical competence for this sort of analysis and negotiation. Yet the stakes are high enough that they might well consider asking a consultant to assist them for a few days over several months.

If the college does decide to attempt a realistic assessment of hardware alternatives, the first step is the request for proposal, a statement for the benefit of potential bidders of what the college wants to buy. The request for proposal must indicate what the complete system should be capable of, but be general enough not to exclude any options that might turn out to be potentially valuable. The following points should be covered:

(1) Hardware requirements. How much work the processor should be able to do in an hour can be stated in terms of some well-known computer, possibly the one the college has presently: three times the throughput capacity of the XYZ/123, for instance. Special devices and capabilities, input and output equipment, storage media (tapes and disks), and the capability for interactive service should all be described if they are to be part of the new system. If the system should be one that can later be expanded or if it should be compatible with some other system, this should also be stated.

(2) Software requirements. The languages, systems, operating system characteristics, and library routines and programs must be spelled out. If some systems are not required but are desirable, it is wise to mention this too. If a computer comes equipped with such languages as APL or ALGOL and if this might affect the decision, it is certainly a good idea to let this be known to those who are offering their systems to the college. An expression of interest in applications programs may also prove worthwhile because, if instructional or administrative programs exist that can be used on the proposed configuration, they could be of considerable value to the college and are worthy of consideration.

(3) Benchmark problems. The college should state its intention to run a series of problems on the proposed computers before a decision is made. These problems are usually called benchmark programs. Several jobs representative of the work anticipated for the system are run on each of the hardware configurations being considered. The time it takes to run these jobs can be used to form a good estimate of the capability of the system to handle the work

load of the college. Also, the ability of the software to accept the inputs of the college without modification can be evaluated. Finally, some other characteristics of the system will probably emerge: arithmetic accuracy in running scientific jobs, the ease of using the system, and so on.

(4) Support services. The need for reliability should be described, including backup for critical administrative jobs, rapid availability of maintenance personnel, and service.

This document is then presented to all interested vendors. Without limiting itself to the hardware of a single vendor, the request for proposal describes what the college wants in a computer as precisely as possible.

*Proposal evaluation.* As a result of this effort, the college should find itself with four or five proposals to evaluate. Because the request for proposal was specific and honest in describing what the college wanted, it should be relatively easy to compare and evaluate the alternatives. Benchmark programs are run and the results evaluated. The proposed hardware and software are compared with the request and each acceptable proposal is graded on how close it comes to the ideal. The reliability of the vendor's support services may be evaluated by talking to some of his other customers: a few phone calls may save the college from painful mistakes and will certainly bolster the confidence of the decision-makers, particularly if they finally decide to select the hardware of a relatively unknown manufacturer.

Finally, of course, the prices of each of the proposed systems are compared. The best is not always the most expensive, but when it is, some soul-searching is necessary. The most attractive of the proposals may also be the most expensive. It can be argued that since this proposal comes closest to the request, it should be accepted. However, further examination may show that for the same cost other proposed systems could be expanded to include new and attractive features, making one of these the most cost-effective choice. Some thoughtful deliberations may be needed to decide whether the additional advantages of the more expensive proposals are worth the additional cost. However, the deliberations are not always this intense and difficult. More often than one would expect, the most attractive proposal is among the cheaper ones, so all that is needed is courage, a conviction that the analyses were made correctly, and the confidence that nothing important was left out.

The top administration often follows these deliberations with less interest than it did the initial effort; after all, these are technical matters with which the president is not concerned. However, when the committee reaches a decision, it is presented to the president for his approval. The report, with its evaluation of the minutiae of the proposals and the details of the benchmarks, does not mean much to the president, and he may be unsure how thoroughly he should try to understand it. He fully accepts the need for the move, which he approved months ago when the requirements analysis was presented to him. But how much should he be concerned with the selection of a particular vendor? If the president trusts the competence of his technical personnel, he probably will give the document his approval after only a cursory glance. But if he fears some controversy about the decision, he may look for an independent evaluation: he may ask a consultant or a trustee or an alumnus with appropriate experience to look at the report and react to it.

*Contract negotiations.* During the evaluation of the proposals a single comparable cost was used for comparing the systems: monthly rental on the basis of a three-year lease, for example. Now, however, it is time to consider seriously on what basis the hardware will be acquired. It can be rented from the manufacturer; it can be purchased outright; a third party can buy the system and lease it to the college. The alternative selected is based on financial considerations, of course; but the important factor in making the decision is the faith the college can place in its own planning. The rental figure from the manufacturer is based on a breakeven time of about forty to fifty months; that is, if the renter keeps the machine beyond that point, he is better off to have purchased it. If the college is confident that its estimates of future needs are correct and that the computer will be retained for longer than this period, then the college should buy the hardware. On the other hand, if there is little confidence that the plan is adequate or if voices on the campus suggest that it will be necessary to revise the plan in two to three years, then rental is the wise choice. The financial vice-president should discuss these matters with the committee and also discuss alternative schemes with representatives of the vendor before deciding how to proceed.

The contract the college eventually signs with the vendor includes a detailed list of the equipment to be supplied and its minimum acceptable performance characteristics. Also included is a list of the software systems to be furnished, with descriptions of the vendor's responsibilities regarding maintenance and training. The document further states that the college will not accept the hardware until it can successfully complete a specified set of acceptance tests, including benchmark programs and some endurance trials. The contract should also specify the maximum number of errors acceptable within an eight-hour period, or some other means of measuring the reliability of the computer.

Acceptance testing serves some valuable functions, although by the time they are performed, the computer is installed on the campus and users have begun writing their programs for it. It is probably too late for anyone to say no. However, the buyer can continue saying not yet until he is convinced that the machine performs according to specifications and is reliable enough to be worth paying for. It is a time when everyone is likely to be nervous: the representatives of the vendor feel responsible for the machine to perform faultlessly because they are the technicians who put it together and because any failure will probably be instantly known to their management; the representatives of the college also feel responsible, for it is they who selected this computer rather than the others proposed.

*The Site.* Once the computer is selected, the problem arises of where to put it when it arrives. The architecture of a computer center should reflect the realities of computer use. This lesson is sometimes learned only after the computer is installed. At Hypothetical University, for instance, the computer was installed in a vacant laboratory in the physical sciences building and caused no end of trouble. Because of the valuable equipment in the building, the doors had been customarily locked in the early evening; but students wanted access to the computer at night. The laboratory soon proved much too small for storing cards and tapes and for users to wait and work in. But no other space could be made available on that floor of the building without moving some other facility.

Exemplary College, on the other hand, is lucky in having an

ugly and out-of-the-way computer center. The building is not im-
posing and not particularly convenient, yet it functions well: there
is easy access for users and such off-campus personnel as maintenance men and delivery trucks; and there is the capability of tight
security to protect a multi-million dollar investment from accident
or malicious mischief, while still permitting easy access to users
nearly twenty-four hours a day.

ADMINISTRATIVE SOFTWARE

Acquiring software entails the same commitment of funds
and plans over a period of years that hardware does. But administrative software also requires new and different behavior from administrative personnel.

When installing administrative computing, the policies and
procedures of the relevant administrative offices must be analyzed,
so that the new system does what the administrators want to have
done and not what some outside agent thinks the administrators
*should* want. At many colleges, this lesson is learned only too late.
The administration pays experts to develop programs, but when the
system becomes operational, the administrators find to their dismay
that using it means completely changing their methods of operation.
Or, worse, they find that the programs simply do not accomplish
the tasks they were designed for. One college, accepting a student
registration system developed for it by a commercial firm, discovered
the system would not register students. The developers, looking over
the disaster area left by the fall registration, claimed that it was not
their fault; students had been careless in filling out their forms. Yet
any system that does not recognize that students (and faculty and
administrators, too, for that matter) sometimes misspell even their
own names is not built to serve a real function at a real institution.

*Defining need.* Meeting one noon in the faculty dining
room, the registrar and the data processing manager of Exemplary
College have lunch together. The registrar says that he has wanted
to ask the manager's advice on the advisability of a new system for
registration and student record-keeping. He cites the difficulties with
the current system and the sort of thing he thinks might be possible.
Together they consider in rough terms the feasibility, possible cost,

and schedule for such a development. As a result, they agree that the subject is worth pursuing. The manager agrees that a systems analyst on his staff can begin spending some time on the registration system within the next week or two. This analyst generates the requirements analysis, the first step in a new system.

The analyst begins by talking with the registrar and the people in his office in order to understand how the current system works, especially with respect to the flow of information: where it comes from, who uses it, how it gets transferred from one document to another, how it is stored, and when (if ever) it is discarded. He assembles a list of all the documents and forms, with information on who handles all of the copies, and why. The analyst next considers the question of what is wrong with this system: what objectives are not being met? Again, he talks with the people concerned, from the students standing in line to the president, who sees only a one-page summary a few days after registration. He discusses with them how they use or create the documents they handle and how these documents could be improved. As a result of these surveys, the analyst eventually is able to produce a document describing the need and what a new system should be able to do. It does not say *how* these objectives will be accomplished, only what they are.

The system analyst then presents this bulky volume of information to the registrar. The Exemplary registrar does not just pass the document on to his assistant (who in turn will give it to his assistant) or approve it unread. He and the key members of his staff read it carefully, marking any passages they find unclear or in error. Because they know that the way their office will function in the future depends on this document, they feel it is necessary to examine it in minute detail now. The system analyst's mistakes, misunderstandings, and poor judgment are the source of the bottlenecks in the system that they will have to live with.

In fact, the chances for mistakes in the system are very great here, perhaps greater than at any later time. Computers rarely make mistakes that cannot be detected and corrected; programs can be tested thoroughly and objectively by people who understand programming and the techniques of error analysis. But an error in design occurs in the no man's land between the technician and the user and each may be relying on the other to find it. Besides, an error in design, undetected and uncorrected now, is all but impossible to fix later. When the system is used on registration day two years hence, the registrar may discover that it is not at all what he had in mind, but what is he to do at this late date? The money has already been spent and the scheduled months have elapsed: it is no longer possible to start over. The registrar will probably try to make do, for rarely is the system totally unusable. Generally, it is considered "good enough," for no one wants to admit having designed or condoned the design of the wrong system. So it is used despite its inadequacies and despite the grumbling of the students who are subjected to it and the clerks who must deal with it. And, if blame must be placed somewhere, it is not placed on the registrar or the analyst, but on "the computer."

The difficulty in assuring adequate analysis of requirements and system design is due to several factors. First, the user, the registrar, does not really know what he wants, at least not in any detail. He is aware that the current system does not work well any more, but he has thought very little beyond this. The analyst must try to get him to be specific and to consider alternatives that may seem very remote at the time of their discussion. Further, the user may know very little about systems and computers and thus have little understanding of what is possible, of what is easy and cheap and what is hard and expensive. Then, too, he has a full-time job managing the current system and this prevents his spending as much time on the new one as he should. Ironically, the more he needs a new system, the more time he is probably required to spend holding the old one together. It is usually all he can do to spare an hour or two a week to talk with the analyst.

The analyst has his limitations too. His profession is systems analysis and design. Since he is concerned with information and the processes described in computer programs, he has only a shallow understanding of the actual use to which his system will be put. He knows in a general way the functions of registration and record-keeping, but naturally views the process as an outsider with his own point of view. He must depend on others to guide him, even though the others do not always appreciate the operational implications of what he is asking them to do for him.

*Evaluating alternatives.* However, once the requirements are well understood, the staff can consider how to develop a system to meet them. Major alternatives include revising the current manual system and introducing new procedures to overcome the present difficulties; adapting the system developed at some other institution to suit the needs of this one; buying an available system from a commercial software vendor; or designing a new system from scratch, either by the college staff or by a commercial agency.

The first alternative means patching up the current system so that it satisfies the requirements enunciated by the system analyst. Perhaps revising the procedures, redesigning the format of some of the forms, or adding a few clerks will solve the problem. If so, a lot of time and effort and money will be saved by not developing a radically different system.

If this is not possible, then perhaps there is a system at another institution that can be transplanted without too much difficulty, saving the cost and time of writing new programs. However, this usually means changing the programs considerably to make them compatible with procedures at this college or changing the practices of the college to make them compatible with the programs. The same is probably true with acquiring a system from a commercial agency, although such programs may have more flexibility. Yet these alternatives are often worth considering, for adapting a solution from another source can save time, money, and effort.

Finally, a system can be custom-built by the technical personnel available at the college or by an outside agency. This is the most expensive and time-consuming alternative, but since it produces a system specifically designed to meet the needs of the users, it has been in the past the option most often selected.

*System design.* If designing a new system is the only feasible choice, the analyst and his associates then describe a system that will satisfy the requirements. The documents they produce specify what the people will do, what the computer will do, the forms to be used and their functions, and the records to be maintained on magnetic computer tape, in five-drawer files, and on microfilm. The documents also include specifications for each of the computer programs, describing the format of the input and output, the language, and sometimes the methods.

The design is based upon the analysis of requirements, on

current practices in the college, and on the ingenuity of the analysts. It should also be based on a review of what other colleges have done in similar circumstances. If the design team has the opportunity to visit other projects, or at least to read descriptions of them, they will be able to incorporate many good ideas that might not otherwise have been considered.

The design documentation should also include estimates of cost and schedule for the implementation of the system, and its cost of operation. When these documents are complete, they are again reviewed in detail by the registrar and his staff. This is the system that they are going to be using; the documents describe the role they are to play and the ways in which the computer will help them. To evaluate the documentation properly, the registrar should ask the following questions and should not permit any further work on the system until they are answered to his satisfaction: Are the middle and lower level administrators convinced that the system will work? Are the costs reasonable, considering the need and the available funds? Is the schedule satisfactory? Can we wait that long? Does it allow for the parallel use of the old and new systems until we are sure the new one will work? Does the plan allow for later modification if errors and omissions are discovered?

*System development.* If the plan, the schedule, and the cost appear satisfactory, the supporting programs are written and tested against the design documents. At the same time, further documentation is produced, describing how the system operates and what various people should do. The system analyst also starts meeting with the staff to review how the system will work and how their routines will change.

At this point in the development of the new registration system at Exemplary College, Miss Crusty, who has handled degree auditing for more than thirty years, realizes that she still does not understand how it will be possible for her to do her work on the basis of the information and files and time she will be given. Her days are full of frustration and anger and her nights are crowded with visions of her thin and helpless body crushed beneath the onrushing army of computers. At last she goes, red-eyed, to the registrar to discuss the possibility of her early retirement. The registrar is less convinced than Miss Crusty of the infallibility of the computer people; he calls the system analyst into his office to ask him how this part of the system is really going to work. After half an hour, they discover that Miss Crusty is right: the system will not allow her to do her job. A modification is made to the requirements document, to the system design document, and to the computer programs.

When the system analyst and his programmers finally tell the registrar that the system is complete, the registrar is as cautious and legalistic as a computer manager when accepting a new machine from an external vendor. The registrar asks for a demonstration of the system on a realistic set of inputs; he asks his staff to review the system one more time to be sure that nothing has been left out; he finally approves its use for fall registration; however, he keeps the old system operational, too—just in case.

In addition to meeting the technical requirements, the people who build the new system, including the registrar, must take care to provide for adequate customer relations, worker relations, and user relations.

The system will work directly with students and faculty, most of whom have had little say in the design of the system or their interface with it. They are the customers of the registrar's services and their needs must be considered as carefully as those of the customers of a commercial venture. If the system does not meet their needs, their hostility to it will make it unworkable and will seriously affect their relations with the registrar.

The clerks and assistants and the middle level administrators must want the system to succeed or it will surely fail. When people at this level refer to a new system as "their" system (meaning that it belongs to the system analyst and the programmers), there is little hope that it will work well; these people are expecting the technical personnel to make it work for them. If they think of it as "our" system and its success is important to them, then it has a chance. If Miss Crusty had waited until the system was operational, she would have had some revenge for her nightmares, but the interests of the college would hardly have been served.

Finally, the system must generate enthusiasm and support from the ultimate users of the system, the registrar and the other administrators, by providing them with useful information.

*Developing the know-how.* When Exemplary College de-

veloped its new registration system, everyone apparently did everything right and no one made any serious mistakes. Nearby Excelsior
College would like to emulate this effort, but it does not have the
experience or the qualified personnel of Exemplary. If they try to
do it, their system will be far too expensive, take much too long,
and probably end up as a botched job. Their first and most important problem, therefore, is how they can develop the capabilities
they need to make good design decisions when they build their new
system. Several steps can be taken. Organizations concerned with
systems in higher education hold meetings annually or even more
frequently. Excelsior should certainly consider sending some of its
people to these meetings. Besides, system analysis and design are not
totally esoteric; there are books and courses available where the
techniques can be learned and practiced. Some of the administrative personnel should be encouraged to take advantage of these op-
portunities. Also, every effort should be made to send visitors to
colleges like Exemplary, to learn what they did and how they did it.
All of these visits need not be to colleges where everything was done
right. A great deal can be learned by talking with people who did
everything wrong, and now know it. They do not usually document
their mistakes but they are generally willing to talk about them. This
will tell the Excelsior people about the dangers to watch for. Finally,
if they feel unsure of themselves when they set out on their venture,
perhaps they should consider hiring a consultant to visit them periodically, note the progress they are making, and comment on it. A
competent professional should not need more than a day or two a
month to keep an eye on the system and to notice potential trouble
spots.

CONCLUSION

As noted at the beginning of this chapter, technical matters
are usually best left to technicians. If the college administrators feel
they cannot trust the technical personnel to make good decisions, the
solution is not to become technicians themselves but to replace the
technicians with people they can trust. However, the administrator
cannot always keep computing technicalities at arm's length. When
a technical decision will affect the life and the finances of the college

for a long time to come, the good administrator will want to get close to the technicalities in order to examine and support the decision.

The administrator must get close to the technical issues when a system is being designed for his use and the use of his staff. The interface between the technical aspects of the process and his own responsibilities is very close here; both he and the technicians must be sure that they understand one another and that they are working together to insure that the result of their cooperation satisfies the requirements.

RESOURCES AND REFERENCES

Many books and articles have been written on the technical aspects of the issues discussed in this chapter. I shall list a few that I think the reader may find valuable if he wishes more information than I have presented. Kanter (1970) is a good, readable text that covers both system development and hardware selection. Joslin (1968) is a detailed study of the processes of computer selection. Mathews (1968), an article that has been mentioned earlier, takes a broader look at the situation and is less technical and detailed than Kanter. Gaunt (1971) has published a series of three brief articles on computer selection. Anyone acquiring computer hardware should consider getting a second-hand computer. *Datamation* (October 1, 1970) devotes several articles to used computers.

Systems development also has a considerable literature of how-to-do-it and how-I-did-it and how-I-should-have-done-it reports. Benjamin (1971) is a relatively brief description in simple terms of the system development process. From among the many good works available, I have selected several other books that repay study: Matthews (1971), Clifton (1970), Shaw and Atkins (1970), and Heany (1968).

# 12

# COMPUTERS FOR
# INNOVATION AND
# SERVICE

"After growing wildly for years," the Pierce Report (President's Science Advisory Committee, 1967) announced in its opening paragraph, "the field of computing now appears to be approaching its infancy." Having advanced beyond early infancy, at least, computing on campus today appears to be playing the two not totally compatible roles of a laboratory for innovation and a factory for service. For one segment of the college community, computing is still an experimental, imaginative, challenging innovation in education. The computer center is an exciting place, a laboratory where new things happen and where the emergence of new vistas results in a constant turmoil of change. But computing has also become essential for performing routine academic

162

work, and the computer center is a shop where people take or send their work to be done. The service provided by the shop must be stable and cheap.

The second of these roles is moving into dominance. Ironically, the success of innovative computing creates the second role and assures its ascendancy. An idea, a method, a machine is invented in a research laboratory. But if it is to pass into general use, it must be transplanted into the environment of the factory—we cannot play with it forever. Computing has proved itself an essential service to education: but essential services can not be supplied by experimental facilities; they must be provided by a cheap and reliable source.

Every educational institution must face the task of identifying such a source of computing for its unique purposes. Each college should decide what computing services it needs and what it can afford to spend for them. The decision can be made either by thoroughly evaluating the situation or by grasping at the first concrete suggestion that comes along. This book has frankly advocated the former course.

Thorough evaluation calls for an analysis of what the users of the service are going to need and what the alternative modes of supply will be able to offer. The range of user needs on a single campus may be very wide; just supplying access to a powerful machine is not enough for any but a small class of users. The range of services is also wide and growing wider, from on-campus hardware, either centralized or distributed, in a number of forms and sizes and from a number of vendors, to off-campus hardware services of several kinds. Software can be acquired from several sources or be made to order on campus. The pairing of needs with potential services and the analyses involved in making a decision about alternatives have technical, political, and financial aspects. It is not easy for any individual on campus to consider all these facets. The decision really requires intimate cooperation between different interest groups and several levels of administration. Not surprisingly, colleges have often chosen to short-circuit this cumbersome process, selecting the first alternative presented or buying the same computer as the college up the road.

An essential ingredient in computing as a laboratory for

innovation was its flexibility. Computing was able to develop to serve the needs of users as they emerged, with little administrative control, and to change its nature and direction as users grew in their understanding of what they wanted to do and changed their own objectives. The large community that now depends on computing, however, does not always find this form of management satisfactory. In fact, managing the computing center like a research laboratory may actually diminish the quality of the service. For example, in a laboratory context the computing is controlled by the users who get there first, so that new and different users are not always well served. Further, such computing lacks the stability essential to routine instruction, research, and administration computing; it provides neither the user nor the supplier with incentives for efficiency; it makes the coordination of divergent groups using the same facility difficult; and it results in an unpredictable demand for a service planned years ahead and fixed in price.

The computer center on a large modern campus has become a business run for the convenience of the academic community at large, resembling the cafeteria or the bookstore more than its advocates care to admit. It hires personnel and buys machines to produce a service. The fact that the college itself runs this business should not obscure the importance of its serving the college expertly and efficiently.

Not all users applaud efforts to control computing for the good of the institution as a whole. Those who have dominated the computing scene are quite naturally afraid that they will lose some of their control and get less of the service. But this control must eventually emerge. It can be accomplished through organization, policy, and planning. Its goal is a system that encourages useful growth but discourages waste, that protects users from one another and from the computing facility management, and that protects the computing management and the service quality from the natural unpredictability of the user community.

The same rational analysis and careful control should apply to the financial aspects of computing. If the college faculty and administration know what their computing dollars are buying and not simply what they are spending, they should be able to evaluate what they need against what they can afford to spend and to weigh computing against alternative means of improving education. If the campus community decides that computing is worth only five dollars or fifty dollars or even one hundred dollars per student, then this must be the decision the college acts upon. The recommendations of experts and statistics about what other colleges are planning to do are irrelevant. Each college must puzzle out its own decision about what computing is worth and what the college can afford to pay for it. Except for relatively small amounts, computing money comes solely out of the institution's own pocket. So if a college wants computing and has to pay the bill, it had better make its own decisions. This is the view at least from the ivy-covered administration building, across the fields and towers, to the chrome and glass of the new computer center. But it is not the only perspective.

From a little further off, it may appear that much of this independence of action is illusory. Colleges are part of a larger system and their future depends on selecting options compatible with other parts of the total system. From this point of view, rational analysis of computing can be pursued by multi-campus groups as well as by a single institution. Perhaps independent action by one institution is a luxury that higher education can ill afford any longer; perhaps computing is a field where coordination and sharing of resources are in order.

Thus resource-sharing becomes a focus of interest affecting hardware services, instructional materials, and administrative systems. Super-centralization provides computing for several colleges from a single source. It can supply to the user more sophisticated computing and a wider range of systems than he might otherwise have access to. For the small college, a regional network can mean expanded access to computing. The potentialities of a national network promise the same expansion to the large research-oriented university. To the agency paying the bill, the sharing of hardware resources may provide greater economy and organization than does independent action.

The development of instructional material using the computer requires time and devotion on the part of talented, skilled people. There are not enough of these people for every department in every college. Thus inter-institutional cooperation is needed to supply good instructional software. This need has implications for hardware services; it favors either super-centralization as a means of supplying such software or the wide acceptance of particular types of mini-computers for particular sets of users. (A chemistry department, for instance, may want to select the computer that many other chemistry departments are using in order to share instructional materials.)

In administration, there is neither money nor time nor the skilled personnel to permit the independent development of high quality software on every campus. Thus cooperation seems the only way for most colleges to apply administrative systems. Because of security requirements and traditions of accountability, an administrative movement toward super-centers, or even toward unified on-campus centers, has not been evident. However, a few major universities are moving in this direction, and many others will undoubtedly follow. Ways of sharing the cost of administrative software are being explored, for there is just no financially acceptable alternative to cooperative effort.

Cooperation and resource sharing in these three areas have increased largely because the national agencies that pay much of the cost of research computing find it attractive. NSF in particular has funded super-centers rather than on-campus computers. The development of a national network by ARPA has also served to bring money, interest, and talent to bear on the sharing of academic computing resources. State systems of higher education, paying the costs of instructional and administrative computing, see the same advantages in resource-sharing as do the sponsors of research. There has thus been a trend in public education toward computing facilities designed to serve the interests of academic users throughout a state system.

But the interest of the institution and its users may also be served by resource-sharing. Many users find access to a network a great asset, for at least part of their requirements. The relatively naive user is able to turn to the regional center for fast education and for immediate access to software. The relatively sophisticated user can gain access to the instructional and research work of his colleagues, to specialized software and special-purpose machines, and to data collections of immense size.

Experimental computing remains important, however, for

computing is still a new idea in education, and despite its high cost and elaborate structures its most important forms and its ultimate applications may yet be unknown. Too much organization and control may stifle the experimentation that permits the emergence of worthwhile ideas incompatible with the existing structure. Computing as a stable service must therefore not totally suppress its disruptive role.

Past experiments in using computers to aid education have resulted in functions that now need to become stable services. But a successful experiment does not spell the end of research; it demonstrates the potential of further experimentation. Thus the structures built around computing must allow innovation to emerge. Excessive zeal to assure the total organization of computing on a campus, regional, state, or even national level is bound to suppress new ideas and new potentialities. Let us be sure that a little freedom, a little anarchy remain. The Rand report discussed in Chapter Nine supported this view in its recommendations that access to computing in education should be available wherever it would be cost-effective and that the cost-effectiveness of education by means of computing should be explored further. That is, educational computing must remain a laboratory for innovation.

The need for continued flexibility in academic computing has another aspect: as computing has matured, the educational vehicles it serves have been demonstrating a potential for revision and renewal. By contributing new possibilities to education, computing has been aiding in its transformation.

Comparing what we can see of the campus of tomorrow with that of today, we note greater access to higher education and a consequently more heterogeneous body of students; more individualized instruction; more relaxed forms of instruction in terms of time, location, and content; more specific definitions of the objectives of instruction and of the proficiency of students. Innovative computing can play an important role in helping colleges come to terms with each of these changes. But how can we prevent experimental computing from being drowned in organization and control? The answer is deceptively simple: unmanage part of it. No matter how large and complete any system may be, part of the community it serves should be permitted to go outside the system to satisfy their needs. This means that part of the money available for computing must be allowed to leak out of the system, a difficult policy to implement or defend. On a small budget, any funds that leak out may threaten the entire system; centralization seems to require the cooperation of everyone on campus. On a larger scale, such a policy may look like deliberate inefficiency. But such a relaxation of control is the only way to protect an immature structure against the institutionalization that would prohibit potentially disruptive developments but which would also stifle developments that might totally overshadow the value of what we have done so far.

Finally, let us take one more look at the campus computing center. What is likely to happen to it? What decisions should be made regarding it? On many campuses, its future must appear very unsure. It operates in an environment of perpetual financial and political crisis. Some see little reason for its continued existence. "We are unstable as hell," one computer center director told me recently. "We have an impossible environment of conflicting demands, rules, and policies. We have to satisfy federal, state, and on-campus administrators who don't understand the first thing about computers. We may have to shut down at any time, and, if we do, centralized computing will be dead on this campus."

And yet, the computing center serves an enduring role. The same director admitted that if his organization does not continue as a physical center and supplier of hardware services, it will continue to exist as a center for the collection and dissemination of information. Such centers are essential, and it seems reasonable to predict that they will exist on every campus. Some on-campus centers will retain their hardware by becoming specialized vehicles for service to a national clientele, offering discipline-oriented computing, for example. Other centers will appear off campus, at national research facilities, to provide these services to on-campus users. Instructors and administrators will probably also take increasing advantage of off-campus service because of the availability of software from regional sources. In public education, state agencies are likely to assume a role in coordinating or directing such resource sharing. In order to attain comparable advantages, private colleges may need to enter into similar alliances.

A national network of these multi-campus service facilities

that will make them available independent of geography seems almost inevitable. They will probably be based on the ARPA network, which has opened the door to a host of possibilities for solving the problems of hardware and constructing the means for communication between many different kinds of computers. It would seem futile to invest time, effort, and money in the construction of a different system that would have to have almost identical ends. If other specialized networks are called for, they will quite probably use the ARPA network as a physical basis.

The individual campus, large or small, at the associate or doctoral level, is thus likely to see intramural computing decline as users find their resources off campus and spend fewer computing dollars internally. The shift from institutional independence to resource sharing is bound to be slow, however, as colleges gradually learn how to share the risks of such a complex and extensive undertaking. Interdependence for an essential service is not easy, and new bridges will have to be constructed.

If this book has a single message, it is that computing must be viewed as an academic resource for serving an integrated and goal-oriented system of education and research. The basic bridges are thus also academic and need not be seen as serving computer traffic alone. They are part of the growing understanding of interdependence in the many and varied interests of colleges and universities.

# LIST OF
# ORGANIZATIONS

AMERICAN ASSOCIATION OF COLLEGIATE REGISTRARS AND ADMISSIONS OFFICERS (AACRAO). One Dupont Circle, Suite 330, Washington, D.C. 20036. AACRAO publishes periodically a survey of computer use in administration, especially in student record applications. The survey is a valuable and interesting review of what typical institutions are doing.

ASSOCIATION FOR COMPUTING MACHINERY (ACM). 1133 Avenue of the Americas, New York, N.Y. 10036. The major association of computer scientists, it maintains special interest groups in many areas. These groups hold meetings (usually in conjunction with the meetings of the parent organization) and publish bulletins that contain valuable and current information. Four of these groups may be of interest to readers of this book: the Special Interest Group for Computer Science Education (SIGCSE), the Special Interest Group on Computer Systems Installation Management (SIGCOSIM), the Special Interest Group on Computer

170

Use in Education (SIGCUE), and the Special Interest Group on University Computer Centers (SIGUCC). Information about them can be obtained from the parent organization.

ASSOCIATION FOR EDUCATIONAL DATA SYSTEMS (AEDS). 1201 Sixteenth Street NW, Washington, D.C. 20036. This association consists of professional educators and technical specialists oriented toward educational applications of computers. It sponsors annual meetings and publishes a journal and occasional special reports.

CONFERENCE ON COMPUTERS IN THE UNDERGRADUATE CURRICULA (CCUC). It is perhaps misleading to call this an organization. It is in fact a series of meetings held annually under this general title. The proceedings of the conferences are published by the organizations that sponsor the meetings. There is no permanent organization. The 1973 meeting is sponsored by the Institute for Educational Computing of the Claremont Colleges, Claremont, Calif. 91711. Since this is the most recent conference planned at the time of this writing, it is probably the best source of further information.

COLLEGE AND UNIVERSITY MACHINE RECORDS CONFERENCE (CUMREC), F. B. Martin, President. 42 Hannah Administration Building, Michigan State University, East Lansing, Mich. 48823. This annual conference is devoted primarily to administrative applications and the problems of administrative data processing management.

COLLEGE AND UNIVERSITY SYSTEMS EXCHANGE (CAUSE). 737 29th Street, Boulder, Colo. 80302. An institution devoted to exchange of information about administrative systems, it sponsors educational seminars and conferences and encourages small groups with special interests to develop within the organization. It also maintains a systems index, which includes information on administrative systems that can be acquired from the colleges where they were developed.

EDUCATIONAL SYSTEMS CORPORATION. Box 2995, Stanford, Calif. 94305. The corporation publishes the *Journal of Educational Data Processing* and some monographs on computers in education.

INTERUNIVERSITY COMMUNICATIONS COUNCIL (EDUCOM). Box 364, Princeton, N.J. 08540. Consisting of institutional rather than individual membership, this organization was formed to encourage interinstitutional cooperation in the development and use of computing. It sponsors two meetings a year and publishes a quarterly *Bulletin* as well as the proceedings of its conferences and some monographs. It has held seminars for administrators on the use of computers in higher education and sponsors a consulting service. Its Educational Information Network (EIN) is a mechanism for sharing programs, primarily in research and instructional applications.

NATIONAL CENTER FOR HIGHER EDUCATION MANAGEMENT SYSTEMS (NCHEMS): see Western Interstate Commission on Higher Education.

SPECIAL INTEREST GROUP FOR COMPUTER SCIENCE EDUCATION: see Association for Computing Machinery.

SPECIAL INTEREST GROUP ON COMPUTER SYSTEMS INSTALLATION MANAGEMENT: see Association for Computing Machinery.

SPECIAL INTEREST GROUP FOR COMPUTER USES IN EDUCATION: see Association for Computing Machinery.

SPECIAL INTEREST GROUP ON UNIVERSITY COMPUTER CENTERS: see Association for Computing Machinery.

SEMINAR FOR THE DIRECTORS OF ACADEMIC COMPUTING CENTERS. Computing Center, University of Colorado, Boulder, Colo. 80302. The University Computing Center sponors this annual seminar and also publishes proceedings following the meetings.

WESTERN INTERSTATE COMMISSION ON HIGHER EDUCATION (WICHE). P.O. Drawer P, Boulder, Colo. 80302. The Program of the National Center for Higher Education Management Systems (NCHEMS) at WICHE is intended to design, develop, and encourage the implementation of management information systems and data bases to encourage better institutional management, more exchange of information, and to facilitate reporting of comparable information. It publishes numerous reports and papers and has produced several computer-based systems that are available.

# BIBLIOGRAPHY

ALPERT, D., AND BITZER, D. "Advances in Computer-Based Education." *Science*, 1970, *167*, 1582–1590.

American Association of Collegiate Registrars and Admissions Officers. *Survey of the Management and Utilization of Electronic Data Processing Systems in Admissions, Records, and Registration, 1969–1970.* Washington, D.C., 1970.

"The ARPA Network." *AFIPS 1972 Spring Joint Computer Conference Proceedings.* Montvale, N.J.: AFIPS Press, 1972.

ASHENHURST, R. L. (Ed.) "Curriculum Recommendations for Graduate Professional Programs in Information Systems." *Communications of the ACM*, 1972, *15*, 363–398.

AUSTIN, J. E. "Planning Computer Services for a Complex Environment." *AFIPS 1971 Fall Joint Computer Conference Proceedings.* Montvale, N.J.: AFIPS Press, 1971.

BAKER, W. O. "Computers as Information-Processing Machines in Modern Science." *Daedalus*, 1970, *99*, 1088–1120.

BENJAMIN, R. I. *Control of the Information System Development Cycle.* New York: Wiley, 1971.

BITZER, D. "The Design of an Economically Viable Large-Scale Com-

173

puter-Based Educational System: Plato IV." *Computing in Higher Education 1971: Successes and Prospects.* Princeton, N.J.: EDUCOM, 1971.

BITZER, D., AND SKAPERDAS, D. "The Design of an Economically Viable Large-Scale Computer-Based Education System." In R. Levien (Ed.), *Computers in Instruction, Their Future for Higher Education.* Santa Monica, Calif.: Rand Corporation, 1971.

BLUM, R. (Ed.) *Computers in Undergraduate Science Education.* College Park, Md.: Commission on College Physics, 1971.

BORK, A. M. "Computer-Based Mechanics." In R. Blum (Ed.), *Computers in Undergraduate Science Education.* College Park, Md.: Commission on College Physics, 1971a.

BORK, A. M. "The Computer in a Responsive Learning Environment— Let a Thousand Flowers Bloom." *Proceedings of the Second Annual Conference on Computers in the Undergraduate Curricula.* Hanover, N.H.: The University Press of New England, 1971b.

BORK, A. M., AND BALLARD, R. "Computer Graphics and Physics Teaching." *Proceedings of the 1972 Conference on Computers in Undergraduate Curricula.* Atlanta, Ga.: Southern Regional Education Board, 1972.

CAFFREY, J., AND MOSMANN, C. *Computers on Campus.* Washington, D.C.: American Council on Education, 1967.

"Campus Computers: Federal Budget Cuts Hit University Centers." *Science,* 1969, *165,* 1337–1339.

CANNING R. G., AND SISSON, R. L. *The Management of Data Processing.* New York: Wiley, 1967.

CLIFTON, H. D. *Systems Analysis for Business Data Processing.* Princeton, N.J.: Auerbach, 1970.

*Computer Aided Instruction and Computer Managed Instruction.* London: British Computer Society, 1971.

*Computer Characteristics Review.* Watertown, Mass.: Keydata Corp., periodical catalog.

"Computer Directory and Buyers Guide." *Computers and Automation,* November 1970, June 1971, September 1972.

*Computers and Computation.* San Francisco: W. H. Freeman, 1971.

*Computing in Higher Education 1971: Successes and Prospects.* Princeton, N.J.: EDUCOM, 1971.

COOLEY, W. W., AND GLASER, R. "The Computer and Individualized Instruction." *Science,* 1969, *166,* 574–582.

COONS, S. A. "The Uses of Computers in Technology." *Scientific American*, 1966, *215* (3), 176–188.

COUGER, J. D. *Computers and the Schools of Business.* Boulder, Colo.: University of Colorado, 1967.

"Curriculum 68, Recommendations for Academic Programs in Computer Science, A Report of the ACM Curriculum Committee on Computer Science." *Communications of the ACM,* 1968, *51,* 151–197. (Also available as a reprint from the ACM.)

"The Dartmouth System and Its Applications." *AFIPS 1969 Spring Joint Computer Conference Proceedings.* Montvale, N.J.: The AFIPS Press, 1969.

*Datamation,* October 1, 1970. Special issue on used computers.

*Datamation,* April 1972. Special issue on networks.

DAVIS, R. M. "Federal Trends Relating to Computing and University Campuses." *Second Annual Seminar for Directors of Academic Computing Centers.* Boulder, Colo.: University of Colorado, 1971.

DE GABRIELLE, C. "The Role of Commercial Time-Sharing Services." In R. Levien (Ed.), *Computers in Instruction: Their Future for Higher Education.* Santa Monica, Calif.: Rand Corporation, 1971.

DE GRASSE, R. V. *Remote Computing in Higher Education: Prospects for the Future.* Burlington, Vt.: The University of Vermont, 1971.

*Digital Computer Needs in Universities and Colleges, a Report of the Committee on Uses of Computers.* Washington, D.C.: National Research Council, 1966.

DITRI, A. E., SHAW, J. C., AND ATKINS, W. *Managing the EDP Function.* New York: McGraw-Hill, 1971.

DONAHUE, J. P., AND MC KINNEY, J. R. "Information Systems for Administrative Control." In A. Knowles (Ed.), *Handbook of College and University Administration.* New York: McGraw-Hill, 1970.

DUGGAN, M. A., MC CARTAN, E. F., IRWIN, M. R. (Eds.) *The Computer Utility: Implications for Higher Education.* Lexington, Mass.: Heath Lexington Books, 1970.

*EDUCOM Bulletin,* 1972, *7* (3). Special issue on teaching computer science.

FARMER, J. *An Approach to Planning and Management Systems Implementation.* Boulder, Colo.: WICHE, 1971.

*The Financing and Organization of Computing in Higher Education.* Princeton, N.J.: EDUCOM, 1971.

FINERMAN, A. (Ed.) *University Education in Computing Science.* New York: Academic Press, 1968.

GAUNT, R. N. "Computer Management." *College and University Business,* April 1971, 74–78; June 1971, 68–70; August 1971, 20–27.

GERARD, R. (Ed.) *Computers and Education.* New York: McGraw-Hill, 1967.

GILLESPIE, R. G. "University/Computer Center Interfaces or One More Bureau in a Bureaucracy." *Seminar for the Directors of Academic Computing Centers, Final Report.* Boulder, Colo.: University of Colorado, 1970.

GILLESPIE, R. G. "Allocation of Resources in a Joint Administrative/ Academic Computing Center." *Second Annual Seminar for Directors of Academic Computing Centers, Proceedings.* Boulder, Colo.: University of Colorado, 1971.

GREENBERGER, M. "The Uses of Computers in Organizations." *Scientific American,* 1966, *215* (3), 192–202.

GREENBERGER, M. "A Quick History of the Development of Computing in Higher Education." *The Financing and Organization of Computing in Higher Education.* Princeton, N.J.: EDUCOM, 1971.

HAMBLEN, J. W. *Computers in Higher Education: Expenditures, Sources of Funds, and Utilization for Research and Instruction 1964–65.* Atlanta, Ga.: Southern Regional Education Board, 1967.

HAMBLEN, J. W. *Inventory of Computers in U.S. Higher Education 1966–67.* Washington, D.C.: National Science Foundation, 1970.

HAMBLEN, J. W. "Using Computers in Higher Education: Past Recommendations, Status, and Needs." *Communications of the ACM,* 1971, *14,* 709–712.

HAMBLEN, J. W. *Inventory of Computers in U.S. Higher Education 1969–70.* Washington, D.C.: National Science Foundation, 1972.

HAMMER, P. C. *The Computing Laboratory in the University.* Madison, Wisc.: University of Wisconsin Press, 1957.

HEANY, D. F. *Development of Information Systems: What Management Needs to Know.* New York: Ronald Press, 1968.

HEFFERLIN, J. B., AND PHILLIPS, E. L. *Information Services for Academic Administration.* San Francisco: Jossey-Bass, 1971.

HOLTZMAN, W. H. (Ed.) *Computer-assisted Instruction, Testing, and Guidance.* New York: Harper and Row, 1970.

HUNT, E., DIEHR, G., AND GARNATZ, D. "Who Are the Users? An Analysis of Computer Use in a University Computer Center." *AFIPS 1971 Spring Joint Computer Conference Proceedings.* Montvale, N.J.: AFIPS Press, 1971.

*Information.* San Francisco: W. H. Freeman, 1966.

JOHNSON, C. B., AND KATZENMEYER, W. G. (Eds.) *Management Information Systems in Higher Education: The State of the Art.* Durham, N.C.: Duke University Press, 1969.

JONES, E. "Resolving Conflicts in the Cooperative Use of a Computer for Research and Administration." *Association for Educational Data Systems Journal,* September 1967, 15–18.

JOSLIN, E. O. *Computer Selection.* Reading, Mass.: Addison Wesley, 1968.

*Journal of Educational Data Processing.* 1971, 9 (1–2).

JUDD, W. "Computer Assisted Instructional Systems for Higher Education: Problems and Prospects." *Computing in Higher Education 1971, Successes and Prospects.* Princeton, N.J.: EDUCOM, 1971.

KANTER, H., MOORE, A., AND SINGER, N. "The Allocation of Computer Time by University Computer Centers." *Journal of Business,* 1968, *41,* 375–384.

KANTER, J. *Management Guide to Computer System Selection and Use.* Englewood Cliffs, N.J.: Prentice-Hall, 1970.

KEHL, W. B. "The Challenge of Financial Responsibility." *Second Annual Seminar for Directors of Academic Computing Centers.* Boulder, Colo.: University of Colorado, 1971.

KNIGHTS, E. M. (Ed.) *Mini-computers in the Clinical Laboratory.* Springfield, Ill.: Charles C. Thomas, 1970.

KOPSTEIN, F. F., AND SEIDEL, R. J. "Computer-administered Instruction versus Traditionally Administered Instruction: Economics." *AV Communications Review,* 1968, *16,* 147–177.

KRUEGER, E. R. "Funding a Computing Center: Color it Green." *Seminar for the Directors of Academic Computing Centers Final Report.* Boulder, Colo.: University of Colorado, 1970.

KRUEGER, E. R. "Fiscal Management of Computing Centers in the 70's." *Second Annual Seminar for the Directors of Academic Computing Centers Proceedings.* Boulder, Colo.: University of Colorado, 1971.

LAWRENCE, B., AND GULKO, W. W. "A National Effort to Improve Higher Education Management." *Journal of Educational Data Processing,* 1971, 9 (1–2), 44–54.

LEKAN, H. A. *Index to Computer Assisted Instruction.* (3rd ed.) New York: Harcourt Brace Jovanovich, 1971.

LEVIEN, R. *Institutions, Innovation, and Incentives.* Santa Monica, Calif.: Rand Corporation, 1971a.

LEVIEN, R. (Ed.) *Computers in Instruction, Their Future for Higher Education.* Santa Monica, Calif.: Rand Corporation, 1971b.

LEVIEN, R., AND OTHERS. *The Emerging Technology, Instructional Uses of the Computer in Higher Education.* New York: McGraw-Hill, 1972.

LYKOS, P. G. "The Computer in Higher Education, A Position Based on Personal Experience." In R. Levien (Ed.), *Computers in Instruction, Their Future for Higher Education.* Santa Monica, Calif.: Rand Corporation, 1971.

MC QUILLAN, J. M., CROWTHER, W., COSELL, G., WALDEN, D., HEART, F. E. "Improvement in the Design and Performance of the ARPA Network." *AFIPS 1972 Fall Joint Computer Conference Proceedings.* Montvale, N.J.: AFIPS Press, 1972.

MATHEWS, M. V. "Choosing a Scientific Computer for Service." *Science,* 1968, *161,* 23–28.

MATTHEWS, D. Q. *The Design of the Management Information System.* Princeton, N.J.: Auerbach, 1971.

MEYERS, E. D. "Project IMPRESS: Time-Sharing in the Social Sciences." *AFIPS 1969 Spring Joint Computer Conference Proceedings.* Montvale, N.J.: AFIPS Press, 1969.

MEYERS, E. D. "IMPRESS and Undergraduate Education in the Social Sciences." *Proceedings of a Conference on Computers in the Undergraduate Curricula.* Iowa City, Iowa: University of Iowa, 1970.

MINTER, J., AND LAWRENCE, B. (Eds.) *Management Information Systems, Their Development and Use in the Administration of Higher Education.* Boulder, Colo.: WICHE, 1969.

MOSMANN, C., AND STEFFERUD, E. "Campus Computing Management." *Datamation,* March 1, 1971, 20–23.

*Networks for Higher Education.* Princeton, N.J.: EDUCOM, 1972.

NIELSEN, N. R. "The Allocation of Computer Resources—Is Pricing the Answer?" *Communications of the ACM,* 1970, *13,* 467–474.

OETTINGER, A. G. "The Uses of Computers in Science." *Scientific American,* 1966, *215* (3), 160–172.

OETTINGER, A. G., with S. Marks. *Run Computer Run.* Cambridge, Mass.: Harvard University Press, 1969.

ORR, W. (Ed.) *Conversational Computers.* New York: Wiley, 1968.

OSBORNE, A. "The Potential Use of Minicomputers in Education." *Journal of Educational Data Processing,* 1971, *8* (6), 1–10.

PARKHILL, D. *The Challenge of the Computer Utility.* Reading, Mass.: Addison Wesley, 1966.

PRENTICE, W. C. H. "Simulating the Financial Future of a Four-year College." *Journal of Educational Data Processing,* 1971, *9* (1–2), 18–21.

President's Science Advisory Committee. *Computers in Higher Education.* Washington, D.C.: White House, 1967.

*Proceedings of a Conference on Computers in the Undergraduate Curricula.* Iowa City, Iowa: University of Iowa, 1970.

*Proceedings of the Second Annual Conference on Computers in the Undergraduate Curricula.* Hanover, N.H.: University Press of New England, 1971.

*Proceedings of the 1972 Conference on Computers in Undergraduate Curricula.* Atlanta, Ga.: Southern Regional Education Board, 1972.

RALSTON, A. "University EDP . . . Get it All Together." *Datamation,* March 1, 1971, 24–27.

RAY, J. L. "The Changing Role of the Service Bureau." *Datamation,* March 1970, 52–54.

"A Report of the ACM Curriculum Committee on Computer Education for Management." *Communications of the ACM,* May 1972, 363–398.

"Resource Sharing Computer Networks." *AFIPS 1970 Spring Joint Computer Conference Proceedings.* Montvale, N.J.: AFIPS Press, 1970.

ROBERTS, M. M. "A Separatist's View of University EDP." *Datamation,* March 1, 1971, 28–30.

ROWELL, H., AND RUTLEDGE, R. "Management Control." *Financing and Organization of Computing in Higher Education.* Princeton, N.J.: EDUCOM, 1971.

SACKMAN, H. *Man-Computer Problem Solving.* Princeton, N.J.: Auerbach, 1970.

SCHIFFMAN, R. L. "The Computer User: A Necessary Evil?" *Seminar for the Directors of Academic Computing Centers Final Report.* Boulder, Colo.: University of Colorado, 1970.

SCHWAB, B. "Economics of Sharing Computers." *Harvard Business Review,* Sept. 1968, *46,* 61–70.

*Second Annual Seminar for Directors of Academic Computing Centers, Proceedings.* Boulder, Colo.: University of Colorado, 1971.

*Seminar for the Directors of Academic Computing Centers, Final Report.* Boulder, Colo.: University of Colorado, 1970.

SHARPE, W. F. *The Economics of Computers.* New York: Columbia University Press, 1969.

SHAW, J. C., AND ATKINS, W. *Managing Computer Systems Projects.* New York, McGraw-Hill, 1970.

SIMON, H. "Computer-Time Allocation." *Science,* 1966. *153,* 122.

SIMON, H. *The Sciences of the Artifical.* Cambridge, Mass.: MIT Press, 1969.

STEFFERUD, E. A. "The Environment of Computer Operating System Scheduling." *Association for Educational Data Systems Journal,* March 1968.

STETTEN, K. J. "The Technology of Small Local Facilities for Instructional Use." In R. Levien (Ed.), *Computers in Instruction, Their Future for Higher Education.* Santa Monica, Calif.: Rand Corporation, 1971.

SUPPES, P. "The Uses of Computers in Education." *Scientific American,* 1966, *215* (3), 206–220.

SUPPES, P., AND MORNINGSTAR, M. "Computer-Assisted Instruction." *Science,* 1969, *166,* 343–350.

SUTHERLAND, I. E. "A Futures Market in Computer Time." *Communications of the ACM,* 1968, *11,* 449–451.

THEIS, D. J., AND HOBBS, L. C. "The Minicomputer Revisited." *Datamation,* May 15, 1971, 24–34.

THEIS, D. J., AND HOBBS, L. C. "Trends in Remote-Batch Terminals." *Datamation,* September 1970, 20–26.

WEEG, G. P. "The Role of Regional Computer Networks." In R. Levien (Ed.) *Computers in Instruction, Their Future for Higher Education.* Santa Monica, Calif.: Rand Corporation, 1971.

WILLIAMS, L. H. "A Functioning Computer Network for Higher Education in North Carolina." In *AFIPS 1972 Fall Joint Computer Conference Proceedings.* Montvale, N.J.: AFIPS Press, 1972.

WITHINGTON, F. G. *The Organization of the Data Processing Function.* New York: Wiley, 1972.

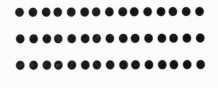

# INDEX